To Teri

From Oppression To Jubilee Justice

Lowell Noble

Lowell Noble

Foreword & Epilogue by John M. Perkins
Poetry by Alexis Spencer-Byers

Jackson, Mississippi

Requests for permission to make copies of any part of this work should be mailed to Permissions Department, Urban Verses, P.O. Box 3583, Jackson, MS 39207

ISBN: 978-1-59526-869-3

Printed in the United States of America by Llumina Press

Library of Congress Control Number: 2007934485

To Dr. Martin Luther King, Jr.,
my posthumous mentor,
and Dr. John M. Perkins,
my living mentor

Table of Contents

Foreword

The prophet, Habakkuk, agonized over the violence, injustice, crime and cruelty in Judah. "Justice is always the loser," he said.

I, too, agonize over the violence, poverty, oppression and crime among my people here in Jackson, Mississippi, and across the country. Justice seems to be the loser among my people also.

Lowell Noble, my colleague for the past ten-plus years, is, like me, horrified by oppression and passionate about justice. For Lowell, Luke 4:18-19 captures the need for the poor to be released from oppression by incarnating Jubilee justice in a community through the power of the Holy Spirit. While this calls for radical changes in the American Church and in American society, nothing less will meet the desperate needs of my people.

Before I turn you over to Lowell, let me share a few of my own thoughts about justice. I'll start with this: if we accept the Bible as the Word of God, then we know He created mankind for His own glory and honor. If we are to bring glory to Him, then we must understand that justice is God's motivation for redemption. The issue we have here is that a holy, unchangeable God has created some beings that are out of control. Now, how can He bring those beings back into His original purpose for them? For God to be just, He's got to remove the curse of sin in order to have relationship with us. So God Himself, by his own sovereign will and action, took upon Himself the curse of sin – the just died for the unjust. Justice, then, becomes God's moti-

i

vation for redemption. So then, in a religion that is about serving God and serving one another, justice should be the most important issue.

Somehow or another, though – maybe because we are human, and we are bent toward injustice, we have removed justice as an important issue. Let's go back to the Old Testament for a moment, to the Law given by God to Moses – the Law was to be the governing force of God as it relates to His redeemed people, who would now be His witnesses in the world. God set up a system, based on His love for humanity, as well as His love for justice. The Law includes this idea of Jubilee – Jubilee justice, to me, is an expression of joy. The joy of obedience, the joy of justice, the joy of redemption. And our joy in justice becomes an act of worship.

So then, the question is, "How do we restore and practice justice in a world, in a society, that is bent on injustice?" This book is an attempt to bring justice back as a central piece of the theology and life of God's people. It represents the struggle to express God's justice in this crooked and perverse world that we live in.

To understand why the evangelical Church in America has separated justification from justice – or, to use James' terminology, to understand why we have been strong on faith but weak on works – we have to take an honest look at ourselves, and at our history. Fundamentally, I believe that people's and communities' own selfish desires cause this division – because if you do justice, you can't exploit people; you can't take advantage of people; you can't have your own selfish, willful way. Doing justice means not just loving God, but also loving your neighbor – all of humanity – *as yourself.* Selfish individualism and justice are inherently incompatible.

If we look back on our history, the accommodation of slavery is one of the main reasons that the American evangelical Church never really gained an anchor in strong biblical justice. Old Testament Jubilee justice provided for the release of those who had fallen into slavery, so again, we had two concepts that could not co-exist, and justice was the loser.

In modern history, we have Karl Marx, his confrontation of the Church, and our reaction to his ideas. From the 1950s on, this country has been moving, with just a little interruption here and there, to a wealth unprecedented in human history. During this same period, Christian colleges made great headway, growing in size and influence. And as the evangelicals went to building their colleges – not only did they not deal with slavery adequately, but they also felt the need to respond to the phenomenon of communism. Communism claimed to build a world based on good works, with some sense of equal distribution of resources. Equal distribution of resources, if that could be achieved, would be justice. The Jubilee, the Sabbatical – those were reckoning days – and it was a reckoning in relation to the poor, people who had gotten in debt, people who had lost everything.

In theory, communism seeks to bring justice through good works and the equal distribution of resources. The Church figured the only way we could confront that was to focus almost exclusively on the spiritual. Our schools, then, did not provide the systematic, practical teaching needed to build good works into our social fabric. We put in how to grow a church, how to tell the world about Jesus, how to evangelize the world – but not how to do justice.

So I think we have to come back and look at that verse in Chronicles – "If my people, who are called by my name, will humble themselves and pray and seek my face and turn from their wicked ways, then will I hear from heaven and will forgive their sin and will heal their land" (2 Chron. 7:14). At any time, in any place, at any time in history, God says He will hear from heaven, and He'll forgive our sins, and He'll heal our land. And so what we have to do, then, is look at our current situation, understand how we got there, and talk about it. We need not to get stuck in the past, but we do have to understand how we got here, in order to repent adequately. Then, and only then, can we start all over again – then we can have what we call renewal, reform, a revival.

Which brings us to a very important question – a question we have to ask whenever we seek to correct something in the Church. Do we love our people, or do we just want to condemn them? Do we want renewal? Is our aim restoration? I know Lowell well, and I assure you that his purpose is not to condemn. The hope of this book is that people who read it will see the importance of bringing justice back to the center of our faith. That we will come to see a commitment to justice not as something extraordinary, but as a basic understanding of the way we ought to live. The further hope is that as we do that, we will experience revival in our nation.

I often quote Micah: "He has showed you, O man, what is good. And what does the Lord require of you? To act justly and to love mercy and to walk humbly with your God" (Micah 6:8). Over the last ten years, Lowell and I have worked closely together in conversation, struggling with and discussing this issue, reading books – what you hold in your hands right now is some of the fruit of that dialog and study. It is a book that modern-day Christians ought to read; it's a book that pastors need to reflect upon; it is a book for teachers, and for anyone who is interested in obedience to the Word of God and heeding Micah's call. I hope and pray that this book will contribute to Amos' idea that justice would roll down like water, and righteousness as a mighty stream.

Dr. John M. Perkins
Jackson, Mississippi
2007

Preface

I am one of them – a white, middle-class, Americanized evangelical. I was converted – born again – in 1949, but I was still blind in one eye, and I did not know it. For 40 years, I remained largely unaware of the Biblical emphasis on social oppression/social justice issues.

Born on an Iowa farm – literally, in a farm house – in 1926, I grew up during the Great Depression. I was a teenager during World War II. Moderate poverty, gas rationing, and tire rationing meant my life revolved around a neighborhood tied to a one-room rural school. Even the 16-mile trip to the county seat, Osage, was a rare event. So I was insulated and isolated from the very poor, other ethnic groups and the urban scene.

It is not easy to overcome 40 years of ignorance, half-truths and indoctrination. It has been a long, slow, difficult pilgrimage to reach some degree of Biblical and sociological awareness of social oppression/social justice issues. I have moved through many stages of understanding – from ground zero to where I am at 81 years of age. At each stage of new insight, I thought that I had finally "arrived," only to soon discover that I still had much more to learn.

I've had to rethink much of what I had previously been taught at church and at Christian liberal arts colleges. On socioeconomic issues, my pastors and professors were where I was – uninformed and ignorant, and they didn't know it. There were huge theological gaps, ideological versions of U.S. history, and sociological blindness that often blamed the victim. Secular sociologists have been ahead of most evangelical Christians on socioeconomic issues.

During your first 40 years, you learn a lot of stuff, some of which you believe deeply, not knowing that a lot of it consists of half-truths posing as the whole truth. Sometimes these supposed truths are almost totally erroneous, based on myths that have been repeated again and again and seem to be true. For example, I was taught that our Founding Fathers were Christians. Some were, but that is not the whole story. Only later did I learn "the rest of the story." The rest of the story is that the Puritans mixed a lot of social garbage with their brand of Christianity; that most of our Founding Fathers were deists, not theists; that they were a white, male, "propertied" elite who discriminated against women, the poor, Native Americans and Afro Americans; and that they believed with religious fervor that the Anglo-Saxon culture/civilization was superior to all others.

To learn new Biblical truths, one first has to dismantle the web of half-truths, and even lies, that have been masquerading as truth. This can be a long and difficult process, especially if your earlier beliefs were religiously sanctioned. Slowly but surely I had to add new pieces to my theology – ethnocentrism, oppression, the poor, justice, the present and social dimensions of the kingdom of God. I had to do the same with American history, which was seldom taught in a way which fully recognized the depth of ethnocentrism and oppression.

In this book you will find me near the end of my pilgrimage. Allow me to identify some key turning points in my conversion to socioeconomic justice. The first was Martin Luther King, Jr.'s tragic assassination in April 1968. The Holy Spirit used this event like a searchlight shining down from heaven upon these United States of America; for the first time, I saw the severity of racism, the **horror of oppression**. The fire of that moment has never dimmed over the years; it still burns brightly in my spirit.

The second person God used to shape my life is John Perkins. Through his writings and example, I have learned much about justice and ministry among the poor. Since my retirement in 1994, my wife and I have been spending around nine months each year as volunteers at the John Perkins Foundation in Jackson, Mississippi.

Also foundational in shaping my new understanding were 20 years spent in the inner city of Jackson, Michigan. During those 20 years, I taught sociology at Spring Arbor College in the white suburbs, but lived and worshipped in the black community in Jackson. Each day, I observed the sharp contrasts between the two communities, a powerful learning experience. At the same time, I was teaching courses such as Social Problems and Racial and Cultural Minorities.

And now I have had 13 years of experience in West Jackson, Mississippi: a poor, black, urban community.

Sometimes my anger at the blindness of the white evangelical church will come through as I challenge us to repent, to change, to cease being a part of the problem. But I hope what will come through even more clearly is a passion for truth, Biblical truth, even though, at times, it will be an unpleasant truth. Evangelicals, of all people, ought to have a passion for all Biblical truth, not a selective list of Biblical truths. I still love the evangelical church, though at times I am so disillusioned that I want to walk away from it.

People were patient with me in my ignorance, so I will try to do the same. And I am convinced that there are many well-meaning Christians who would "do right" if someone would show them the way. Possibly this book will shed some light on the path toward a more complete understanding of God's will for His people.

A new friend of mine, Lowell Hagan, read the first draft of three chapters in this book. He commented that I write in the "white heat of moral outrage." He was afraid that this intensity, even if true, would end up alienating too many readers that I want to reach. His critique is valid.

So I face a dilemma. Tone down the passionate intensity and reach more people, or, in the tradition of Amos and other Old Testament prophets, speak the truth, as I understand it, and trust

God to help those readers "with ears to hear" receive and act on that truth? I just read an article in *Christianity Today* entitled "Passion Takes It Higher." According to the article, young evangelicals are developing a passion for God, a passion for worship, a passion for Biblical truth. One student, Taylor Dodgen, claims, "We're the generation who likes things raw and uncut and really in-your-face."[1] Taking a look at the unvarnished Biblical truth about oppression and justice will be a good test of that commitment. It is true that InterVarsity and other groups are successfully exhorting their young people to take on tough challenges such as ministry in the world's slums. And I offer my own testimony that those of us who are older, and therefore more steeped in traditional ways of thinking about spiritual issues, still have the potential to embrace a new understanding of the heart, purposes and kingdom of God.

I recall reading someone's comments on Karl Marx's *Communist Manifesto*; he said Marx wrote with a pen dipped in molten anger. Doesn't a Christian, a child of the God who "loves justice" (Isaiah 61:8), have the right to be as angry at injustice as an atheist? Don't answer that question yet – first, read this whole book, as difficult as parts of it may be. Then, send me an email or participate in our online forum (http://www.urban-verses.com/O2JJ/), and tell me whether or not you think I'm justified in being grieved and angry about the ways that professed Christians have ignored such central themes of God's Word.

A few notes about the organization of this book. Logically, it could have been divided into two parts: part one, a Biblical analysis of social oppression and social justice; part two, a modern American application of these Biblical concepts.

I chose a different organizational strategy because I am writing to white evangelicals, most of whom are at the beginning stages of thinking about the gospel socially. Therefore, I inter-

---

[1] Collin Hansen, "Passion Takes it Higher," *Christianity Today* Apr. 2007: 28.

weave the Biblical analysis and the modern application in each chapter so the reader will immediately catch the relevance of the Biblical concepts.

Of these Biblical principles, I have placed a special emphasis on oppression. Why? Because the Biblical concept of oppression is almost entirely missing from evangelical theology and preaching, even though it is a major Scriptural theme. Because of this omission and ignorance, I introduce the reader to the concept of oppression in three different chapters, each time probing the topic more thoroughly.

Another concept that I will introduce is what I call "the American trinity": individualism, materialism and racism. If the book were to be twice as long, I should devote another three chapters to this phenomenon, one to each of its three elements. Since the book is designed to be a short introductory essay, there will necessarily be topics that are discussed at less length than they deserve. I encourage you to engage in further study of these concepts.

As you explore these issues, I again encourage you to visit our online forum and submit an article to stimulate further discussion. You might disagree with something I've said, or you might agree but want to add something, or you might have a question you'd like to hear others address – whatever the case, I hope you'll add your voice to the conversation. Let me share a couple of examples of what I mean. One young person told me that racism is no longer a burning issue for her generation. She would replace racism in the American trinity with nationalism. Someone else told me that he would insert militarism into the American pantheon. I invite these persons and others with different perspectives to share their thoughts in an ongoing dialog around these issues.

It is also my hope that some young theologian will expand my ideas into a full-fledged theology of society. Or that someone will write a full book on the Spirit, the Kingdom, and justice; in my opinion, this theme is a huge missing link in evangelical theology.

Before I send you into Chapter One, I want to take a moment to express my gratitude to two fellow pilgrims who have contributed to this book. I already mentioned how instrumental John Perkins has been in helping me to study and learn about justice issues. I am delighted that he has contributed a Foreword and an Epilogue to this volume. Alexis Spencer-Byers represents a younger generation of justice-minded Christians; she edited my text and also wrote the poems you will find at the end of each chapter.

Now, I invite you to begin reading in earnest; as you do so, please keep in mind that this book is just one small step in your journey. I pray that you will begin to ask God, even now, how you can take what you learn and apply it to the world and church you live in.

Chapter One

Introduction

I have come to see in deeper ways the implications of my faith…
I can no longer proclaim the Cross and the Resurrection without
proclaiming the whole message of the Kingdom [of God]
which is **justice for all.** (emphasis added)
Billy Graham, Transformation, Jan-Feb, 1989

Seek first the **kingdom of God** and its **justice.**
(Mt. 6:33, NEB)

Oppression smashes the body and crushes the human spirit.
Thomas Hanks, God So Loved the Third World

I would like to begin this book with a true story from the life of
Fannie Lou Hamer, the Mississippi-born-and-raised civil
rights activist. The oppression described occurred in the 1920s,
during the segregated era of Mississippi history:

> My parents moved to Sunflower County when I was two
> years old. I will never forget one day when I was six years
> old and I was playing beside the road. This plantation owner
> drove up to me and stopped and asked me, 'could I pick cot-
> ton?' I told him I didn't know and he said, 'Yes, you can. I
> will give you things that you want from the commissary
> store,' and he named things like crackerjacks, and sardines –
> and it was a huge list that he called off. So I picked 30 pounds
> of cotton that week, but I found out what actually happened
> was he was trapping me into beginning the work I was to
> keep doing and I never did get out of debt again. My parents
> tried so hard to do what they could to keep us in school, but

1

school didn't last four months out of the year and most of the time we didn't have clothes to wear.[2]

The plantation owner must have had no conscience to begin the process of exploitation with a six-year-old child! Next Hamer describes how rough life was for her mother because of oppression and poverty:

> I used to watch my mother try and keep her family going after we didn't get enough money out of the cotton crop. To feed us during the winter months mama would go around from plantation to plantation and would ask the landowners if she could have the cotton that had been left, which was called scrappin' cotton. When they would tell her that we could have the cotton, we would walk for miles and miles in the run of a week. We wouldn't have on shoes or anything because we didn't have them. She would always tie our feet up with rags because the ground would be froze real hard. We would walk from field to field until we had scrapped a bale of cotton. Then she'd take that bale of cotton and sell it and that would give us some of the food we would need.
>
> Then she would go from house to house and she would help kill hogs. They would give her the intestines and sometimes the feet and the head and things like that and that would help keep us going. So many times for dinner we would have greens with no seasoning and flour gravy. Sometimes there'd be nothing but bread and onions.[3]

What are conditions like in the Mississippi Delta not quite 100 years later? These *Wall Street Journal* headlines from 1989 give us an idea: "River of Despair: Along the Rich Banks of the Mississippi Live Poorest of U.S. Poor; They Endure a Lack of

---

[2] *Mississippi Writers*, ed. Dorothy Abbot (Oxford, MS: University Press of Mississippi, 1986) 10.

[3] Abbot 11.

Jobs and Plantation Mentality, While Landowners Thrive; Where Dreams of Blacks Die."[4]

One premise of this book is that the blatant oppression of the more distant past has contributed greatly to the economic disparities of the recent past and the present day. Many white evangelicals try to separate these two phenomena, but I believe that not only is it unrealistic to do so, it is also inconsistent to be outraged about the one while simply accepting the other. I hope that you will bring along the emotional response that you had to the descriptions of how Hamer and her family were treated as we discuss current social justice issues, such as the wealth gap.

What is the wealth gap? Thomas Shapiro, in his book, *The Hidden Cost of Being African American*, states that the White/Black wealth gap is 10 to 1[5]. In other words, the average Euro-American household has 10 times the wealth/assets of the average Afro-American household. The wealth/assets gap is both significantly wider than the income gap and more important in terms of overall long-term quality of life.

A more recent study from the Pew Hispanic Center asserts that the Euro/Afro wealth gap is 14 to 1, and that the Euro/Hispanic wealth gap is 12 to 1.

A 2 to 1 wealth/assets gap would be bad, unfair, but a 10 (or more) to 1 gap is outrageous, horrible, obscene. I write this book specifically to my fellow white American evangelicals to sensitize all of us to this terrible fact and to issue a clarion call to act, to do justice. To paraphrase a civil rights chant, "Do justice, white evangelical, do justice."

A few white evangelicals, such as Mary Nelson, Jim Wallis, Bob Lupton, Wayne Gordon, Shane Claiborne and Ron Sider,

---

[4] Dennis Farney, "River of Despair," *The Wall Street Journal* (Vol. LXX, No. 254) 19 Oct. 1989.

[5] Thomas Shapiro, *The Hidden Cost of Being African American: How Wealth Perpetuates Inequality* (Oxford University Press, 2004) 5.

to name a few, are on the frontlines, even in the trenches, waging the battle against injustice. But for the most part, we evangelicals are unaware or in a state of denial or only lightly engaged in the battle for economic justice.

Can we become radically Biblical; can we move beyond an Americanized Christianity? The command to love our neighbor as ourselves includes a call to do justice, to reduce economic disparity. In terms of socioeconomic issues (e.g., oppression, justice, etc.), there is both a theological and a behavioral crisis in the American evangelical church. In this introductory chapter, I will document the need for revolutionary change, change that will go far beyond even the remarkable achievements of the Civil Rights Movement.

As I begin to write this book, it is February, 2007 – Black History month. So I shall start with a quotation from Dr. Martin Luther King, Jr. Almost everyone is familiar with King's eloquent and inspiring "I Have a Dream" speech delivered in 1963. But few know of his "I Live a Nightmare" speech delivered after civil rights legislation had been passed. The nightmare speech was given in December, 1967, four months before his assassination in April, 1968. From a dream to a nightmare – listen to King's haunting words:

> In 1963…in Washington, DC…I tried to talk to the nation about a dream I had had, and I must confess…that not long after talking about that dream I started to see it turn into a nightmare…just a few weeks after I had talked about it. It was when four beautiful…Negro girls were murdered in a church in Birmingham, Alabama. I watched that dream turn into a nightmare as I moved through the ghettos of the nation and saw black brothers and sisters perishing on a **lonely island of poverty in the midst of a vast ocean of material prosperity**, and saw the nation doing nothing to grapple with the Negroes' problem of poverty. I saw that dream turn into a nightmare as I watched my black brothers and sisters in the midst of anger and understandable outrage, in the midst of their hurt, in the midst of their disappointment, turn to misguided riots to try to solve that problem. I saw that dream turn into a nightmare as I

4

watched the war in Vietnam escalating. Yes, I am personally the victim of deferred dreams, of blasted hopes.[6] (emphasis added)

Increasingly King spoke as a prophet of judgment as he saw America doing little to respond to the desperate economic straits of black Americans. While King never forsook his principles of love and nonviolence, he sounded more and more like a revolutionary. Toward the end of his short life, King said that for years he labored "with the idea of reforming the existing institutions of the South, a little change here, a little change there." After years of significant but slow progress, King concluded: "I think you've got to have a **reconstruction of the entire society, a revolution of values.**"[7] (emphasis added)

I think that if King were alive today, he would still be talking about "**a lonely island of poverty in the midst of a vast ocean of material prosperity.**" What is the evidence of a continuing nightmare today? Here are some recent statistics[8]:

* Federal poverty figure for a family of four is around $20,000/year.
* Extreme poverty figure for a family of four is around $10,000/year.
* Number of poor in the U.S. is around 36,000,000
* Number of extreme poor is around 16,000,000
* Number of persons without health insurance is 47,000,000
* For over two decades the U.S. has had the highest (or near highest) percentage of poor people when compared to 31 other developed countries.

---

[6] James Cone, *Martin & Malcolm & America: A Dream or a Nightmare* (Maryknoll, NY: Orbis Books, 1991) 89.

[7] Stephen Oates, *Let The Trumpet Sound* (New York: New American Library, 1982) 441-442.

[8] From *Luxembourg Income Study*, 2006.

Lowell Noble

Why haven't we white evangelicals been vocal and active in the pursuit of economic justice for all? More and more evangelicals are adding ministry to the poor to their agendas, which is good, but is it good enough, Biblical enough? Or are we engaging in limited efforts while at the same time maintaining our white privilege, our white wealth? We need to move beyond charity to justice, beyond reform to revolution, beyond change to transformation, beyond the excuse, "You will always have the poor with you" (John 12:8) to the ambitious, Biblical goal of "There was no poverty among them" (Acts 4:34).

Why is the white evangelical church not fully engaged in sharply reducing the rich-poor gap? May I present one fundamental reason?

The American church, yes, even the Bible-believing, born-again, evangelical church, has usually served two trinities at the same time, often unaware that they are doing so: the Christian trinity of Father, Son and Holy Spirit, and the American trinity of individualism, materialism and ethnocentrism (racism). On Sunday we worship the Christian trinity, but during the week we live by the American trinity. Our behavior is not much different from other Americans.[9]

I would like to elaborate a bit on one dimension of the American trinity: materialism. Recently I read a small book by Scott MacLoed, entitled *Snakes in the Lobby*. MacLoed is a musician and songwriter. He describes a vision he had:

> I was standing in a well-known hotel lobby, which I had literally stood in earlier that same day during a very well-known Christian music conference. In the vision the very large and open lobby was packed full... Many were artists, musicians or people directly involved in the business of music... Much to my astonishment and horror, I saw what looked like a massive snake lying on the lobby floor...

[9] Bryant Myers, *Walking With the Poor: Principles and Practices of Transformational Development* (Maryknoll, NY: Orbis Books, 1999) 189.

6

Amazingly, people were actually leaning up against it! ...no one else seemed to notice it – they just carried on with their business. Many people were surrounded, and some were even totally wrapped up in its monstrous coils, and yet they were still unaware. They were all in great danger... It seemed almost welcome here... The oversized snakes were everywhere... I knew immediately that the great snakes I had seen in the vision were the principalities and dark power (or evil spirits) that have been controlling and manipulating much of Christian music.[10]

Then MacLoed was given an interpretation of his vision. The biggest snake's name was self-promotion. Other snakes' names were lust, pride, insecurity, fear of man, jealousy, etc. One white snake with a light that radiated from it was called religion. In the presence of this white snake "everything looked normal in the lobby – orderly and prosperous. People were smiling, gracious and respectable. There was no sign of trouble."

A spirit told MacLoed, "This is a Christian function. Everything that is done here is done in the name of Jesus, and even for Jesus." MacLoed explains, "This was none other than the voice of 'Religion,' the same power that had gone against my Savior..." There were also snake-keepers in the lobby; they fed the snakes money. This reminded MacLoed of Mt. 23:25-26, where the religious leaders of his day were condemned by Jesus because they were "full of greed and self-indulgence."

I cannot prove that MacLoed's vision is valid, but my sociological and Biblical study leads me to a similar conclusion. In Jesus' day, the real enemy was not Roman oppression, as most Jews concluded (Jesus never railed against Roman oppression); rather, it was a degenerate Jewish religion led by a corrupt religio-politico-economic elite. In America, the real enemy is not secular humanism, as many Christians assert; in actuality, it is the church comfortably co-existing with the American trinity

---

[10] Scott MacLoed, *Snakes in the Lobby* (North Carolina: Morningstar Publications, 1997) 47.

7

of individualism, materialism and ethnocentrism. This American trinity is the snake in our midst.

Early in the history of America, the Puritans began mixing the two trinities. Being British, they were skilled at using religious rationalizations to cover their ethnocentrism and oppression. The British perfected this blending of religion and ethnocentrism/oppression against the Irish and then transported it, lock, stock and barrel, to the 13 colonies. As time passed, to the Puritans, Native Americans became as Canaanites: people to be destroyed in order to make way for a new Christian nation, New England.

The Bible-believing Puritans sanctified the abuse of religion, paving the way for other Americans to use it to legitimate Westward expansion (ethnocentrism and oppression). They claimed it was "God's will" to exterminate and replace the heathen, inferior people who stood in the way of Manifest Destiny.

As I have studied and observed American Christianity and the religion of the Pharisees, I have concluded that our behaviors are frighteningly similar in the area of socioeconomic issues. Luke describes the Pharisees as ones who "neglected justice," as "lovers of money" who pursued "greed and wickedness." Most American evangelicals fit this description as they chase the American Dream; in fact, they often perceive the American Dream as somewhat complementary with the kingdom of God. There are many exceptions to this rule, but the general pattern is far from Biblical Christianity.

How did all this begin in the white European Christian church? *Sojourners* magazine describes a blending of trinities during the slave trade era in an article entitled, "The Miracle at Accra."[11] The World Alliance of Reformed churches had recently met in Accra, Ghana. On their agenda was a continuing and controversial item: a Christian evaluation of the world's economic system. Third World Reformed Christians wanted to

---

[11] Rose Marie Berger, "The Miracle at Accra," *Sojourners* Jul. 2005: 32-36.

condemn the world's economic system as "empire," meaning imperialism, domination and exploitation. Western Reformed Christians refused to flatly condemn an economic system that had been so good to them. It had provided them with prosperity, so how could it be a monstrous evil? Even after much theological reflection, the group was still at an impasse.

Someone arranged for the delegates to make a trip to the Ghana coast to visit a slave dungeon. This was where slaves were held until a slave ship came by to pick them up. The delegates were shocked when they saw that a **Reformed church had been built on top of the slave dungeon.** One delegate recalled, "And we imagined Reformed Christians worshipping their God while directly below them, right under their feet, those being sold into slavery languished in the chains and horror of those dungeons."[12]

As I read this article, the following image flashed through my mind:

Worship God on Sunday,
Trade slaves on Monday.
Worship God on Sunday,
Trade slaves on Monday.

This was the rhythm of life that went on for many years.

After viewing this tragic corruption of Christianity, the Western Reformed Christians finally agreed with the Third World Reformed Christians that the world's economic system was imperialistic, that it was a system of oppression.

Slavery/colonialism was replaced by neo-colonialism. Third World countries gained their political freedom, but the economic system continued to supply the West with cheap raw materials. Even today, this economic system contributes much more wealth to the West than the West gives back in aid. So for about 400 years, the prosperity of the West has been built, in part, on ethnocentrism and oppression.

---

[12] Berger 34.

In February 2007, the movie, *Amazing Grace*, was released. This film portrays the remarkable story of William Wilberforce. It took Wilberforce and his team of allies 20 years to abolish the slave trade and another 26 years to abolish slavery in the British empire. The movie tells a powerful story of dedication to a just cause.

Yet Wilberforce only went halfway. We needed a "Wilberforce II" to complete the task – to move beyond **freedom to justice.** The slave traders and slaveowners were allowed to keep the massive wealth that they had accumulated from this nefarious evil. In fact, the slaveowners were given reparations to compensate them for the loss of their property. The slaves were not given reparations for their years of free labor. **Justice would have required massive redistribution of ill-gained wealth, but instead white wealth was preserved and black poverty reigned.**

Much the same happened in this country. A combination of abolition activism, the Civil War and the Emancipation Proclamation finally freed the slaves. Many Christians were involved in the abolitionist movement.

Freedom opened the door to a glorious, but brief, Reconstruction period. Freedom had destroyed slavery, but not racism. Racism soon reared its ugly head again in the form of neoslavery – segregation and sharecropping.

Freedom was not followed by justice. (Legislation had been introduced in Congress to give each former slave family "Forty Acres and a Mule," but it was never passed.) Freedom without justice is a hollow victory. Freedom without justice meant that freedom itself was soon lost. It took nearly another 100 years before freedom was regained through the Civil Rights movement.

What might have happened had **freedom and justice been combined** in the 1860s? We do have a brief historical example of what could have been, what should have been a turning point in U.S. history.

When General Grant conquered Vicksburg, he confiscated the nearby Jefferson Davis plantation. Grant loaned the freed slaves the supplies to plant a crop. The freed slaves then worked hard, produced a good crop, paid Grant back the loan, and made a profit. Grant was impressed, so he expanded the experiment the next year with the same success. Given half a chance, the freed slaves showed that they could be self-supporting, that they could take control of their own lives.

By military order, Grant had temporarily taken a large justice step, making agricultural land available to former slaves. But the freed slaves did not *own* the plantation. After the war, the plantation was given back to the Davis family as an act of reconciliation between the North and South. A nice gesture, but it left the freed slaves landless in an agricultural society.

And, as mentioned above, Congress did *not* pass proposed "Forty Acres and a Mule" justice legislation. Had they done so, the whole history of the South, and especially Afro Americans, would have been radically different. Had Christians understood the need for justice and pushed as aggressively as some pushed for abolition, maybe, just maybe...

Ivory Phillips is an expert in Afro-American history. On June 30, 2006, during a workshop at the John Perkins Foundation, Phillips gave a lecture comparing the Reconstruction period to the Civil Rights movement. In summary, he stated that both the Reconstruction period and the Civil Rights movement gained a measure of political freedom and civil rights for Afro Americans. But they did not produce economic equality or economic justice. Never in their 400 years in America have Afro Americans as a people gained anything approaching economic justice.

When the white community experiences economic prosperity, the black community experiences an economic recession. When Whites are in an economic recession, Blacks are in a depression. When Whites experience an economic depression, Blacks are in the throes of an economic disaster.

From Historical Past to Sociological Present

How does the historical past haunt the sociological present?

I am an enthusiastic supporter of Christian Community Development (CCD) *à la* John Perkins and his colleagues. These Christians combine evangelism and church with social jus-

11

tice/reconciliation to rebuild poor communities. John Perkins is an optimistic, creative person with a message of hope, love and reconciliation, and he has inspired many to engage in CCD-type ministry across the nation. Yet what Perkins wrote about the nature and causes of poverty and racism in Mississippi in the 1960s remains largely true in our country today. (See Chapter 10 of his *A Quiet Revolution*.)

After discussing individuals in poverty, John examines the cycle of poverty and communities of poverty. Then he moves on to a level of analysis most American Christians avoid. Perkins concludes that the social evils of poverty and racism are deeply ingrained in the **cultural values and social institutions** of American society. It is hard for most white, middle-class evangelicals to accept what Perkins has to say because these same cultural values and social institutions have been good to them. How could they be bad for Afro Americans? Perkins states:

> First, I began to see plainly how sin had organized itself into **structures and institutions of inequality and oppression**... I became acutely aware, as I began to ask the question, "How can we deal with the roots of poverty?" that the roots of poverty were in the system itself, growing out of the very **culture and traditions and history of the South and America.** Paul's words came alive to me, "We are not contending against flesh and blood, but against the principalities, against the powers, against the world rulers of this present darkness, against the spiritual hosts of wickedness in the heavenly places" (Eph. 6:12).[13] (emphasis added)

How do the principalities and powers operate? By incarnating themselves in the cultural values and social institutions of a society. Perkins continues:

> I could see how racism and violence in individuals with power could work their way through the basic institutions

---

[13] John M. Perkins, *A Quiet Revolution* (Pasadena, CA: Urban Family Publications) 88.

of society, and then how self-interest, especially economic self-interest, had led white people in Mississippi to develop structures to control the system and then to justify the enslavement of black people.[14]

With John Perkins' perspective in mind, we can turn to an analysis of contemporary American society. America is a great nation with many strengths and serious weakness.

Positives	Negatives
1. Freedom/democracy	1. High divorce rate
2. Productive economy	2. High crime rate
3. Abundant natural resources	3. High alcoholism rate
4. Quality private and public colleges and universities	4. When compared with 19 industrialized countries, the U.S. ranks first (worst) in 21 social problem categories[15]
5. Highly churched when compared to Europe	
6. Unparalleled set of Bible schools, Christian liberal arts colleges and universities, and seminaries	

---

[14] Ibid.

[15] Andrew Shapiro, *We're Number One* (Vintage Books, 1992). The U.S. is number one in real wealth, number of billionaires, big homes, defense spending, etc. The U.S. is also number one (first meaning worst) when compared to nineteen major industrialized countries in incarceration rate, murder rate, reported rapes, robbery rate, garbage per capita, children and elderly in poverty, homelessness, wealth inequality, divorce, infant mortality, etc. The U.S. ranks last in spending on the poor.

7. A host of parachurch organizations designed to meet specific needs	

This total set of U.S. strengths is unparalleled in the history of the world, especially the Christian strengths. Our Christian schools graduate thousands of well-trained leaders in the areas of business, education, social work, ministry, etc. each year. These Christian leaders should be a massive "salt and light" influence in our society. As a result, the U.S. should, theoretically, have comparatively few social problems. Yet the reality is quite different. When compared with other educated, industrialized countries, we have the **worst social problems record.** One other confirmation of the above comes from the 23-year project by the *Luxembourg Income Study* that compares poverty and income data among 31 developed countries. Citing the Luxembourg Study, the Jackson *Clarion Ledger* recently reported that "over the last two decades, the United States has had the highest or near-highest poverty rates for children, individual adults and families."[16]

Strangely, most of the European countries have a comparatively low rate of social problems, and these same countries have comparatively few active church members. The U.S. has a relatively high church attendance and a high rate of social problems.

Michael Emerson and Christian Smith, in their groundbreaking book entitled *Divided by Faith*, suggest one reason for the existence of this serious disconnect between an apparently robust evangelical faith, on the one hand, and massive social problems, on the other hand. Based on late 1990s data, acquired through a nationwide survey of self-identified evangelicals, Emerson and Smith describe a highly individualized, privatized

---

[16] Julianne Malveaux, "Extreme poverty rises," *The Clarion-Ledger* 12 Mar. 2007.

faith that lacks the "cultural tools" or Biblical concepts to think or act intelligently on social problems.[17]

I would like to challenge our hundreds of Bible schools, Christian liberal arts colleges and universities, and seminaries to become involved in solving four crises damaging our Afro-American community today. I have already introduced one of these crises, the wealth/assets gap.

A second crisis, according to Cornel West and Ronald Potter, is the **loss of hope, the lack of meaning or the spirit of despair** that is widespread among poor urban youth. This hopelessness often leads to seething anger, the disrespect of women and the devaluation of life itself. Alex Gee and John Teter, authors of *Jesus and the Hip-Hop Prophets*, describe the pain and loss of many urban youth:

> Living reckless means you sometimes have to say goodbye early. Real life is full of guns, fights, going before judges, drunk driving accidents and senseless deaths. I know what loss is all about. Burying your friends before they are eighteen will do terrible things to your soul. It is hard to stay positive when your entire world is negative.[18]

Bakari Kitwana, in his book, *The Hip-Hop Generation*, describes the many interrelated crises "that threaten the very future of African American life":

> Leading the list is America's unfulfilled promise of equality and inclusion. Great disparities in education, housing, healthcare, employment opportunities, wages, mortgage loan approval, and the like persist. Collectively, these disparities have profoundly impacted our generation, though

---

[17] Michael Emerson and Christian Smith, *Divided by Faith: Evangelical Religion and the Problem of Race in America* (London: Oxford University Press, 2000).

[18] Alex Gee and John Teter, *Jesus and the Hip-Hop Prophets* (Downers Grove, IL: InterVarsity Press, 2003) 79.

we have lived our entire lives in post-segregation America... The many side effects of the ever-looming war on
drugs, the escalating tensions between young Black men
and women, and the great intergenerational abyss, dubbed
the generation gap, pose an array of previously unseen
challenges in African American life.[19]

The third crisis is in the area of **gender relations**. Orlando
Patterson, historical sociologist at Harvard, has examined the
gender relations crisis in depth in his book *Rituals of Blood*. His
lengthy essay is entitled "Broken Bloodlines: Gender Relations
and the Crisis of Marriages and Families Among Afro-
Americans." Patterson believes that the gender relations crisis is
the number one internal problem facing the Afro-American
community today. He claims that:

> There is a crisis in nearly all aspects of gender relations among
> **all classes** of Afro-Americans, and it is getting worse... Afro-
> Americans have the lowest marriage rate in the nation, and
> those getting married have the highest divorce rate of any ma-
> jor ethnic group. The result is that most Afro-Americans,
> especially women, will go through most of their adult lives as
> single people.[20] (emphasis added)

Then Patterson writes a most tragic paragraph:

> The simple, sad truth is that Afro-Americans are today the
> loneliest of all Americans – lonely and isolated as [an ethnic]
> group; lonely and isolated in their neighborhoods, through
> which they are often too terrified to walk; lonely as house-
> holds headed by women sick and tired of being "the strong
> black woman"; lonely as single men fearful of commitment;

[19] Bakari Kitwana, *The Hip-Hop Generation* (New York: Basic
Books, 2002) 8.
[20] Orlando Patterson, *Rituals of Blood: Consequences of Slavery
in Two American Centuries* (Washington, DC: Civitas Counterpoint, 1998) xi.

lonely as single women wary of a "love and trouble" tradition that has always been more trouble than love.[21]

The fourth crisis is the **massive imprisonment of young black males.** Criminal justice statistics, if taken as an accurate picture, paint a dismal portrait of young black men as highly criminal. But to some extent these "facts" are a result of racial profiling. A case in point: Maryland State Police were engaging in racial profiling in order to stop drug trafficking. Robert Wilkins' legal team did some research to prove their case against the police. They discovered that:

> When they [the Maryland State Police] searched [cars] of a hundred blacks and a hundred whites, they found drugs exactly the same number of times, but they were searching seven hundred blacks for every one hundred whites, so the arrest statistics made it look like seventy percent of the people being arrested for drugs were African American, and then they use those statistics to justify focusing on the African American.[22]

Sociological studies have also indicated that Blacks and Whites use and sell drugs at approximately the same rate. This was found to be true in this case involving the police. If the Maryland State Police had used racial profiling in reverse, and zeroed in on Euro Americans, they could have produced arrest statistics that would make it appear that Euros were trafficking in drugs at seven times the rate of Afro Americans. Then Euro Americans would be filling our prisons, not Afro Americans.

Jerome Miller, in his hard-hitting book entitled *Search and Destroy*, argues that American society uses the criminal justice

---

[21] Patterson xii.

[22] Kenneth Meeks, *Driving While Black: What To Do If You Are a Victim Of Racial Profiling* (New York: Broadway Books, 2000) 10.

system to "solve" many of its social problems. No other modern nation imprisons such a high percentage of its population, largely from minority ethnic groups.

At the request of a federal judge, Miller monitored jail overcrowding in Duval County, Florida, from 1989 to 1994. This gave him first-hand access to the:

> ...written police summaries of each arrest, as well as to the individual criminal histories of those being arrested. The stories that emerged from reading files, counting heads, and interviewing those who sat in jail challenged the stereotypes of the predatory and violent black man as typical of those who people the justice system. That system seemed to be disproportionately concentrating its considerable power on African-Americans charged with relatively minor offenses. The best face one could put on these patterns was that the criminal justice system was being inappropriately applied to the wide range of personal and social problems that affect the cantankerous poor and minorities. It all gave validity to sociologist John Irwin's unhappy characterization of jails as places of 'rabble management.'[23]

Our "war on drugs" has been focused on the poor and minorities, especially black men. What is the direct impact of massive imprisonment?

> In 1992, the NCIA [National Center for Institutional Alternatives] conducted a survey of young African-American males in the Washington, D.C. justice system. It found that on average in 1991, more than four in ten (42%) of all the 18-35-year-old African-American males who lived in the District of Columbia were in jail, in prison, on probation/parole, out on bond or being sought on arrest

---

[23] Jerome Miller, *Search and Destroy: African-American Males in the Criminal Justice System* (Cambridge: Cambridge University Press, 1996) 15.

warrants. On the basis of this 'one-day' count, it was estimated that approximately 75% of all 18-year-old African-American males in the city could look forward to being arrested and jailed at least once before reaching age 35.[24]

These four continuing problems plaguing the Afro-American community have their roots deep in American history, beginning with the ethnocentric Puritans and our rich founding fathers. For documentation, read the following: G.E. Thomas, "Puritans, Indians, and the Concept of Race," *New England Quarterly*, March 1975; *Racist America* by Joe Feagin; *The Wells of Democracy* by Manning Marable; *Before the Mayflower* by Lerone Bennett; *A Different Mirror* by Ronald Takaki; *Race and Manifest Destiny* by Reginald Horsman; and *Myths America Lives By* by Richard Hughes.

Other crises could be added to this list, such as quality of education, sub-standard housing or the lack of adequate health care. In addition, ethnic groups other than Afro Americans have their own unique sets of problems that need to be addressed, but I will not discuss them here. (Please visit our online forum at http://www.urban-verses.com/O2JJ/ to read essays concerning issues faced by other minority ethnic groups, and to participate in discussions around these topics.)

American evangelicals wield significant political influence. We elected a president. My question to us now is this: "Will we become equally passionate about changing our society by adding justice for the poor to our list of moral values?"

"Let **justice** flood the land
(and wash away poverty and oppression)."
Amos 5:24 (Noble paraphrase)

---

[24] Miller 21.

The Island

I can see it all around me
The sparkle and shine
Of more than enough

At times I can even touch it
A big-screen TV
For $10 a week

But if I stop to do the math
The waters recede
And I'm alone on the sand
Watching the little I had
Wash away with the tide

Two Horrendous Social Evils: Luke 4:18 and Luke 4:25-30

I think you've got to have a reconstruction of the entire society,
a revolution of values.
Dr. Martin Luther King, Jr.

The Israelites groaned in their slavery...
God heard their groaning
Exodus 2:23-24

There are two great social evils that are highlighted by Jesus in Luke, chapter four. These two social evils are also prominent in the rest of the Bible and in the history of the world, including in the history of these United States of America. But they are seldom preached about from the white evangelical pulpit. This seems strange to me, since we evangelicals claim to believe the Bible from cover to cover. Why, then, do we neglect these two major Biblical themes? Is it because our hands are dirty?

These two very important social evils are **oppression and ethnocentrism.** First, Jesus mentions oppression in Luke 4:18: he has been anointed "to release the oppressed." Jesus was reading from Isaiah 61 in the Jewish synagogue at Nazareth, but Isaiah 61 does not contain this phrase "to release the oppressed." Jesus goes out of his way, back to Isaiah 58:6, to add this phrase to the key verse in Luke. Why? To highlight the fact that oppression is the primary, though not the only, cause of poverty.

The word oppression occurs about 120 times in the Old Testament, but only about four times in the New Testament, depending on your translation. However, once a person is sensitized to the meaning of the word from the Old Testament references, one can see that the concept of oppression is widespread in the New Testament as well. See, for example, James 5:1-6, a powerful passage that condemns oppression (i.e., mistreatment of workers, including unpaid wages and even murder) though the word is not used.

Karen Lebacqz, in her Harvard doctoral dissertation on justice, claims that all the best western scholars on justice did not really understand what justice was. Why? Because they did not begin with injustice and oppression. Evangelical theology has almost totally ignored oppression; therefore, it has a shallow understanding of justice, another major Biblical theme.

I often ask people if they have ever heard a full-length sermon on oppression. Only one out of 20 says yes. I have asked about 40 students who attend Christian liberal arts colleges if any of their Bible professors have ever taken one class period to discuss in some depth what the Bible teaches on oppression. Not a single hand has been raised. American Christian ignorance on oppression is massive, with tragic consequences. American evangelical Christians have often been oppressors or tolerated oppression. I suppose we don't want to preach on the sins, the evils that we are often engaged in or benefit from. The fact is, we benefit from the wealth gap, of which oppression has been a major cause.

For example, I was born on an Iowa farm that has been in the Noble name since 1896. The Nobles did not take the farm directly from Native Americans. Someone else did that about 50 years earlier. But this fine farm has given the Noble family a good standard of living for more than 100 years. Our present white privilege is built on the back of previous oppression.

In Exodus, chapter six, God speaks directly to Moses, clearly and powerfully declaring to Moses the He **will** deliver the children of Israel from their bondage of slavery, that He **will** take them to the Promised Land, etc. Moses repeats these great promises to the Israelites. Listen to their tragic response:

> Moses reported this to the Israelites, but they did not listen to him because of their discouragement [broken spirits] and cruel bondage (Ex. 6:9).

Oppression, generations of constant oppression, had crushed them, broken their spirits, so they could not believe in God's promises.

My wife's closest Afro-American friend has a grandmother who does not believe in God. She saw and experienced so much oppression during segregation that she cannot believe. Many Native Americans are so broken in spirit because of generations of poverty and oppression that they drown themselves in alcohol.

Yes, I realize that some people, in the midst of their oppression, do, out of their desperation, turn to God, so theoretically all oppressed people could do so. But please do not use this argument to avoid the **horror of oppression.** Oppression does crush many people's spirits; they do fall into a spirit of despair.

The tragedy is that you and I do have an answer, a Biblical answer, but we won't get close enough to the oppressed that we can love them deeply enough and long enough for them to feel our God through us. Why do we evangelicals fail to study God's teaching on oppression and fail to deliver God's answer to oppression – justice – to those who have been crushed?

I live in West Jackson, an inner-city, impoverished, almost exclusively black area in Mississippi's capital city. For many urban youth, life has lost meaning, purpose and hope. Why not eat, drink and be merry, for tomorrow I will die or go to prison? Why not drown myself in drugs or sex? There is no hope. Nobody cares, it seems.

To begin to understand Biblical teaching about oppression, we must look at the way Jesus opened his public ministry in the synagogue in Nazareth (Luke 4:18-19):

> The **Spirit** of the Lord is on me,
> because he has anointed me
> to preach good news to the **poor.**
> He has sent me to proclaim freedom for the prisoners
> and recovery of sight for the blind,
> to release the **oppressed,**
> to proclaim the year of the Lord's favor [**Jubilee justice**].

This brief passage contains four principles that Jesus identifies as central to His purpose, but which are too often neglected in the evangelical church. Evangelicals are strong on a John 3:16 gospel – a personal sin, personal salvation gospel based on the cross and the resurrection – but they are weak on a Luke 4:18-19 gospel.

The four key Biblical concepts highlighted in these verses are: **the Spirit, the poor, the oppressed, and Jubilee justice** (year of the Lord's favor). In the full Nazareth sermon, including 4:25-30, we find a fifth concept – **ethnocentrism.** Ethnocentrism comes from the Greek word *ethnos,* meaning people, nation or culture and often translated Gentile. Ethnocentrism means the supposed superiority of one people/culture, and the supposed inferiority of another people/culture. The Jews thought that they were superior to Samaritans and Gentiles.

Also implied are several other concepts. Alongside the poor are the **rich**; commonly, the rich oppress the poor. And if there are oppressed people, there must be **oppressors** – the religio-politico-economic elite. Two more concepts are presented indirectly. If the poor are released from oppression by incarnating Jubilee justice in a community, then a measure of **shalom** has been achieved. If a community has experienced both John 3:16 and Luke 4:18-19, if a community has achieved both justice and shalom, then the **kingdom of God** is here on earth. Healthy communities are impossible to create unless all of these Biblical concepts are addressed.

An urgent appeal to evangelicals: Why don't we finish what the Civil Rights movement began by adding Luke 4:18-19 to our gospel?

Now, more on ethnocentrism from Luke 4:25-30. In sermon B (sermon A is found in 4:18-22), Jesus tells and interprets two familiar Old Testament stories: Elijah feeds a starving widow, and Elisha heals a leper. Why does this almost get Jesus killed? As Jesus interprets these stories, we find Elijah walking by starving Hebrew widows to reach a starving Gentile widow. And we find Elisha walking by Hebrew lepers to heal a Gentile leper. We see that God's grace was generously extended to Gentiles.

At this time in Jewish history, Jews had turned God into their own private God. Their God was not, could not be, the God of the heathen, unclean Gentiles. Jews had strayed from their earlier high calling: they were a chosen people called to bless all nations by bringing the Messiah into the world. They were to be a servant people, but they had misused their chosenness and turned it into a sense of superiority – ethnocentrism. According to William Barclay, Jews held an "immense contempt for the Gentile." Gentiles were made "to be fuel for the fires of hell." It was not lawful for a Jew to "help a Gentile mother giving birth." And "marriage with a Gentile girl meant the funeral of the Jewish boy."[25] So for Jesus to teach that God was equally concerned about Gentiles was heresy to the Nazareth Jews. Heretics should be killed, so they tried to throw Jesus over a cliff. Ethnocentrism almost resulted in the ultimate act of oppression – murder.

Now, let us examine another example of ethnocentrism in Luke 9:51-54. Jesus was walking from Galilee to Jerusalem – a three days' walk. As he journeyed through Samaria, he and his disciples had to find a place to stay overnight. Jews despised Samaritans, and many Samaritans returned the favor. This particular village would not let them stay overnight.

---

[25] William Barclay, *By What Authority?* (London: Darton, Longman, Todd LTD, 1958) 40.

This refusal infuriated James and John. Earlier in the chapter (9:1-2), they and the other disciples had been given power and authority "to drive out all demons and to cure diseases...and preach the kingdom of God." So they asked Jesus' permission to call down fire from heaven and destroy this impertinent Samaritan village – men, women and children. Had Jesus nodded his head, the Samaritan village would have evaporated into thin air. But instead, Jesus sternly rebuked his disciples, using the same word he had used earlier (9:42) when he rebuked an evil spirit.

Ethnocentrism is indeed an evil "spirit" and should be rebuked. Note that it was Jesus' own disciples who were ethnocentric. Their ethnocentrism led them to want to misuse God's power to kill people. Once again, ethnocentrism nearly led to the ultimate act of oppression – murder.

Teachers know that rebuke should never be the final word in a situation. Occasions for rebuke are potential golden teaching moments. Jesus, the Master Teacher, turned this near tragedy into a positive by following it with the story of the Good Samaritan. For James and John, the phrase "Good Samaritan" was an oxymoron. They hated the Samaritans; they had just tried to destroy a Samaritan village. But Jesus makes the Samaritan the hero of the story. The Samaritan was the one who loved his neighbor, a Jewish neighbor at that.

Future preachers, don't preach the story of the Good Samaritan without contrasting it with the Samaritan story in chapter nine. This vivid contrast will double or triple the impact of preaching a sermon on the Good Samaritan.

Once we begin to understand Biblical teaching about oppression and ethnocentrism, we need to internalize these principles. About 10 years ago, I presented a workshop at a Christian Community Development Association convention. I included about 10 minutes on justice and righteousness. After my presentation, a sharp, thirty-something, Afro-American woman came up to talk. She was leading a CCDA youth organization and working on her doctorate. She said she wept as she listened to my comments on justice and righteousness. She had been hungering in her spirit for some instruction on these themes.

I told her that she did not yet own these concepts; she had heard my talk about them and was helped. But she needed to take another step in order to own them. I happened to have with me a copy of Isaiah's verses on oppression, justice, righteousness and shalom – four pages of verses. I handed her a copy and said, "Carry this with you for the next year, and read and reread these verses in context every spare moment that you have for the next year. Then you will gain a deep understanding of these concepts, and they will be something you own, not just something I have taught you." She returned to the convention the next year and reported that she had done what I had told her to do. This new understanding had revolutionized her life, and she had gone to her adviser and requested permission to make changes in her doctoral dissertation.

If you wish to do the same, find an NIV concordance; copy all the verses on oppression, justice, righteousness and shalom; and study them in context until you can think like an Old Testament Hebrew. Then bring this new understanding with you into the New Testament, and it will revolutionize your understanding of the kingdom of God.

A second-best approach would be to buy a copy of *Kingdom Ethics,* by Glenn Stassen and David Gushee. Stassen and Gushee understand the kingdom of God to be grounded in the book of Isaiah. Isaiah exposed the evils of idolatry and oppression, and he called for justice and righteousness. Only when a community rejected the former and embraced the latter could it experience shalom. The authors move on to the Sermon on the Mount and show the application of Isaiah to the kingdom of God ethic – how the Sermon contains not just principles, but transforming initiatives which form the basis of a social ethic. Stassen and Gushee summarize the seven marks of God's reign from Isaiah as follows:

> *Deliverance* or *salvation* occurs in all seventeen deliverance passages in Isaiah; *righteousness/justice*

occurs in sixteen of the passages; *peace* [shalom] in fourteen; *joy* in twelve; *God's presence as Spirit or Light* in nine… *healing* occurs in seven.[26]

Then the authors assert that Romans 14:17 is a summary of Isaiah's messianic passages. My paraphrase of Romans 14:17 is as follows:

> The kingdom of God is…justice, *shalom* and joy in the Holy Spirit.

Joseph Grassi, a Roman Catholic New Testament scholar, also grounds his understanding of the kingdom of God and justice in Isaiah. See his fine book entitled *Informing the Future: Social Justice in the New Testament.*[27]

Now, let us look directly at Isaiah's Messianic passages; this may be the first time the reader has seen all the Messianic passages together on one page. I urge you to study them carefully, possibly even memorize them, then write a one-sentence definition of the kingdom of God based solely on these passages; use them to articulate a clear and compelling vision of the kingdom of God.

Messianic Passages from Isaiah

9:7   Of the increase of his government and *shalom* there will be no end. He will reign on David's throne and over his kingdom establishing and upholding it with *justice* and *righteousness*.

11:1-4   A shoot will come up from the stump of Jesse; The Spirit of the Lord will rest on him –

---

[26] Glenn Stassen and David Gushee, *Kingdom Ethics* (Downers Grove, IL: InterVarsity Press, 2003) 25.

[27] Joseph Grassi, *Informing the Future: Social Justice in the New Testament* (New York: Paulist Press, 2003).

the Spirit of wisdom and understanding...
with righteousness he will judge the needy,
with justice he will give decisions for the poor.

16:5   In love a throne will be established...
one from the house of David who seeks justice
and speeds the cause of righteousness.

28:16-17 I lay a stone in Zion...a precious cornerstone...
I will make justice the measuring line
and righteousness the plumb line.

42:1-4 Here is my servant...my chosen one...
I will put my Spirit on him and he will bring justice to the nations...
In faithfulness he will bring justice to the nations.

61:1-4 The Spirit of the Sovereign Lord is on me,
because the Lord has anointed me to preach good news to the poor,
to proclaim freedom and release by practicing Jubilee justice for the poor,

to bestow on the poor
a crown of beauty instead of ashes,
the oil of gladness instead of mourning,
a garment of praise instead of a spirit of despair.

These transformed poor will be called
oaks of righteousness or trees of justice.

These transformed poor will rebuild the ruined cities. (Noble paraphrase)

61:8   For I, the Lord, love justice.

Lowell Noble

U.S. History: Puritans and Anglo-Saxons

In a review article entitled "Jonathan Edwards: American Augustine," George Marsden describes pastor Edwards as a deeply spiritual person, a "theological genius." "Edwards was a Puritan absolutely preoccupied with the centrality of God." Dozens of books and more than 75 doctoral dissertations have been written about Edwards, indicating his widespread influence in American religious history.

But Marsden also points out some serious flaws. "Even though he proclaimed spiritual equality, the idea of social equality hardly occurred to him. He owned African household slaves, as was common among the New England elite." Edwards even went down to Providence, Rhode Island, and personally picked out a slave for purchase.

Marsden also notes that Edwards was an "elitist. God had ordered everything and had ordered it as hierarchies." [28] To an elitist, this social order may have seemed logical, natural and normal. But the oppressed see things differently. They see this supposedly God-legitimated social order as evil. Even though cloaked in theology and spirituality, this elitist social order was, in reality, too often an arrogant ethnocentrism which led to acts of oppression against Native Americans. Social oppression/social justice issues, central to the Bible, were not important to Jonathan Edwards.

Edwards died in 1758. During the previous century, the Puritans had settled and developed New England, a land they believed God had given them to develop as a Christian nation. And the Puritans saw themselves as chosen by God to purify a decadent church, apparently completely unaware of their own areas of decadence. We will visit this type of deception again in the chapter on deception versus truth.

Were the serious ethical flaws mixed with Edwards' profound thoughts his own, or were they part of the Puritan heritage handed down to him?

---

[28] George Marsden, "Jonathan Edwards: American Augustine," *Books and Culture* Nov/Dec 1999: 11.

Allen Carden, an evangelical American historian and expert on the Puritans, has documented with great thoroughness the religion and life of the Puritans during the 1600s. Most of his book is devoted to the theology and practice of the Puritans, how they grounded their ideas in the Scriptures. Topics such as human nature, sin, Christ, the covenant, holiness, the kingdom, preaching and piety are comprehensively discussed.[29]

The Puritans attempted to be a profoundly Biblical people, yet they were more selectively Biblical than they realized. They thundered against personal sin, but they were strangely quiet about social evils such as inequality, ethnocentrism and oppression. Does this sound hauntingly familiar, like too many of today's evangelicals? Maybe history does repeat itself. When social evil benefited the Puritans, they found ways to rationalize it as good or at least necessary.

Cardin reveals both the good and bad sides of the Puritans, though he is overwhelmingly positive. But the negative critique is serious indeed. One might expect godless communists to be ethnocentric and oppressive, but Bible-believing Christians??? Among their own people, Puritans had a strong community emphasis based on the idea of the covenant, but this ideal of community was so narrowly conceived that Puritans as a whole were "found wanting in missionary zeal." The "city that was set on a hill" was primarily concerned about its own, and even here social inequality was legitimated as divine social order.

Outsiders – non-Puritans – were not loved as neighbors. Afro Americans and Native Americans were not regarded as equals. As the Puritans wanted more land, conflict developed. Understandably, Native Americans did not want to give up their precious land. So, at times, Puritans resorted to force, killing at least 500 men, women and children on one occasion – a massacre. "The Puritans viewed such 'successes' as com-

---

[29] Allen Carden, *Puritan Christianity in America* (Grand Rapids, MI: Baker, 1990).

31

ing from the hand of God."[30] As Puritan numbers grew, they came to see the Indians as heathen, savage "Canaanites" that were to be destroyed because they stood in the way of the chosen people of God.

The Puritans pursued both good and evil with fervor, certain that they were doing the "will of God." Kevin Phillips claims that no other group pursued their goals with such relentless zeal.[31] It seems that they pursued personal righteousness and ethnocentrism/oppression with equal zeal. Did the Bible Belt of the American South repeat Puritan history?

Modern evangelical Christians have been "especially influenced by the Puritans," both for good and bad. We too have mixed personal piety with ethnocentrism and oppression. Unfortunately, the Puritan pattern of mixing religious piety with oppression has dominated much of American history. The Puritans themselves needed more purification; a brand of the gospel that does not make oppression and justice central theological concepts may itself end up perpetuating oppression and injustice.

An Anglo-Saxon ethnocentrism was blended with this zealous, religious Puritan emphasis. Anglo-Saxonism began as a cultural/civilizational superiority, but in this country it slowly took on a strong racial tone. Reginald Horsman has examined in exhaustive detail the origin and development of "racial Anglo-Saxonism" in *Race and Manifest Destiny*.[32] In essence, Horsman argues that the American brand of racism was developed as a rationalization/justification for Manifest Destiny – the belief that it was God's will for our so-called superior Judeo-Christian heritage to spread from coast to coast and also impact the rest of

---

[30] Carden 109.

[31] Kevin Phillips, *The Cousins' Wars: Religion, Politics and the Triumph of Anglo-America* (New York: Basic Books, 1999).

[32] Reginald Horsman, *Race and Manifest Destiny: The Origins of American Racial Ango-Saxonism* (Cambridge, MA: Harvard University Press, 1981).

the world. Manifest Destiny was supported by a religious, political, economic, cultural and even linguistic sense of
superiority which justified the oppression of any ethnic group
that stood in its way. It legitimated cruel slavery; the near geno-
cide of Native Americans; and oppressive, imperialistic
expansion against Mexico, not to mention Hawaii and the Philippines.

This Anglo-Saxonism was more secular in nature than religious, but it was often believed with religious-type fervor. The
idea of a distinct Anglo-Saxon race/culture has no basis in fact;
it is an ideological myth. But this myth took hold as if it were
fact. The people of England, in reality, were a mix of original
Celtic tribes, Germanic tribes, Viking settlements and Norman
conquest. There is no pure sense of Teutonic or Aryan roots.
Horsman asserts:

> By 1850 a clear pattern was emerging. From their own suc-
> cessful past as Puritan colonists, Revolutionary patriots,
> conquerors of a wilderness, and creators of an immense mate-
> rial prosperity, the Americans had evidence plain before them
> that they were a chosen people: from the English they had
> learned that the Anglo-Saxons had always been peculiarly
> gifted in the art of government [democratic institutions]; from
> the scientists and ethnologists they were learning that they
> were a distinct Caucasian race, innately endowed with abili-
> ties that placed them above other races…they were
> descendants of those Aryans who followed the sun to carry
> civilization to the whole world.[33]

Benjamin Franklin, George Washington and a host of other
colonial leaders drew on and glorified their Anglo-Saxon past,
but it was Thomas Jefferson who drew most heavily on the
ideas of the radical Whigs who had argued that the original
Saxons "had lived under laws based on the natural rights of
men," but "after 1066 these rights had been eroded by the impo-

---

[33] Horsman 8.

sition of kings, clerics, lawyers, and by the whole system of feudalism."[34]

Jefferson was fascinated by everything Anglo-Saxon, including the language; he wrote a simplified grammar of it. He included Anglo-Saxon as a part of his University of Virginia curriculum because:

> As the histories and laws left us in that type and dialect, must be the textbooks of the reading of the learners, they will imbibe with the language their free principles of government.[35]

Jefferson's intense interest in all things Anglo-Saxon "continued throughout his life." The ideal Anglo-Saxon England that Jefferson believed in was a land of small political units and a land in which local rule prevailed in most concerns. "In its early form there was an elective king, annual parliaments, a system of trial by jury, and land held fee simple." Horsman states:

> This view of Anglo-Saxon England was in its way as unreal as those writings which pictured Arthur's England as a Camelot of brave knights, but it persisted in English and American thinking long after Jefferson's death.[36]

Fiction, fantasy became fact, truth. In the year 2000, as I listened in the home of a relative to a pastor's biased version of American history as a part of God's plan, I was reminded again of the power of a myth repeated again and again until it takes on the force of truth. This pastor seemed to believe this false view of American history with about the same fervor as he believed the Bible.

In summary: **the myth of being from a race/culture of superior qualities** (Anglo-Saxon) **was blended with the myth of being a chosen, superior people** (Puritan). **False history and**

---

[34] Horsman 11.
[35] Horsman 12.
[36] Horsman 13.

false biology mixed with faulty theology to create a zealous, militant, and arrogant ethnocentrism/nationalism which led to oppression carried out in the name of God.

Is the U.S. Army a Model?

Can these dangerous ideological myths be broken? Can we chart a new direction? Strange as it may seem, the U.S. Army may be showing us the way to go. Charles Moskos (Euro-American sociologist) and John Butler (Afro-American sociologist) have written *All That We Can Be: Black Leadership and Racial Integration the Army Way*.[37] Both authors served in the military, and both have done extensive research on the military.

In the 1970s, according to Moskos and Butler, "racial strife…had reached epidemic proportions." Some of the top brass believed that the viability of the Army as a functioning military force was at risk. Something had to be done, so the Army "made a decision to do whatever was necessary to achieve substantially full integration and extensive if not completely equal opportunity." As of the 1990s, "not only is the Army a thoroughly integrated institution, its members seem at peace with the idea."[38]

How has the Army moved so rapidly from severe conflict and tension to significant harmony, a large measure of equal opportunity, an unusual degree of Afro-American leadership, and an Afro-Anglo culture, whereas civilian society and the Christian church lag far behind? What are the secrets to the Army's high degree of progress and success (note I did not say perfection) in improving ethnic relations, and can their philosophy and methods be transferred to civilian society and the church?

---

[37] Charles Moskos and John Butler, *All That We Can Be: Black Leadership and Racial Integration the Army Way* (New York: Basic Books, 1996).

[38] Moskos and Butler 8.

Moskos and Butler answer a resounding, *"Yes!"* *If* civilian society and the church want it **badly enough** to make improved ethnic relations and opportunities a **high priority**. This means more than high-sounding rhetoric or feel-good brotherhood meetings. It means a long-range commitment with adequate resources and top-quality personnel to get the job done. We will have to move beyond rigid ideological positions and rhetoric to new language, new concepts and new goals. Rethinking much of what many of us now believe will be the order of the day. New ways of doing things will have to be accepted by both Blacks and Whites.

Moskos and Butler claim that much of America's ethnic discourse on "race" is dominated by "the paradigm of black failure" or a "relentless negative picture of black America."[39] By contrast, listen to their description of the U.S. Army today:

> It is an organization unmatched in its broad record of black achievement. It is a world in which the Afro-American heritage is part and parcel of the institutional culture. It is the only place in American life where whites are routinely bossed around by blacks.

The authors describe the Army's culture as a

> multiracial uniculture... this uniculture is Afro-Anglo – [and it] has been an unquantifiable contributor to its success in race relations. American society sorely needs some similar amalgamation of the two dominant cultures.[40]

In most university dining halls, one sees a self-imposed segregation, but in an Army dining facility, Blacks and Whites commingle by choice. The same commingling takes place in the

---

[39] Moskos and Butler 50.
[40] Moskos and Butler 51.

rest of Army life. "Even off duty and off post, far more interracial mingling is noticeable around military bases than in civilian life." Moskos and Butler freely admit that the Army is "not a racial utopia," but Blacks are "three times more likely to say that race relations are better in the Army than in civilian life."[41]

While the Army clearly opposes discrimination, its primary focus has been to open "avenues that promote black achievement rather than on the rhetoric of non-racism."[42] Afro Americans are 13-14 percent of the American population, but they make up 27 percent of all Army personnel.

Moskos and Butler summarize the lessons of the Army experience:

> Race relations can best be transformed by an absolute commitment to nondiscrimination, coupled with uncompromising standards of performance. To maintain standards, however, **paths of opportunity** must be created – through education, training and mentoring – for individuals who otherwise would be at a disadvantage. We would suggest another lesson as well: there must be enough blacks in the system.[43] (emphasis added)

The book, *All That We Can Be*, ends with a lengthy and convincing discussion about how civilian society could do much the same. One way would be to set up a national service program for young people in which the Army principles would be implemented. The authors list twelve steps or principles to follow:

1. Blacks and Whites will not view opportunities and race relations the same way.
2. Focus on Black opportunity, not on prohibiting racist expression.

---

[41] Moskos and Butler 52.
[42] Moskos and Butler 60.
[43] Moskos and Butler 65.

3. Be ruthless against discrimination.
4. Create conditions so that White and Black youth can serve on an equal basis to improve their social and civic opportunities.
5. Install qualified Black leaders as soon as possible.
6. Affirmative action must be linked to standards and pools of qualified candidates.
7. Affirmative action must follow a "supply-side" model, not a "demand-side" model.
8. A level playing field is not always enough.
9. Affirmative action should be focused on Afro Americans.
10. Recognize Afro-Anglo culture as the core American culture.
11. Enhancing Black participation is good for organizational effectiveness.
12. If we do not overcome race, American society may unravel.[44]

Two questions for consideration:

1. Can or will the church apply these Army principles to move from being the most segregated institution in American society to the most reconciled institution? Will we do it in 25 years?
2. How can other ethnic groups be fit into this new paradigm?

Suggestion: after some preliminary discussion and an iron-clad commitment to justice and reconciliation, call in Moskos or Butler as a consultant.

Although addressing the deep-seated social evils of ethnocentrism and oppression cannot be done easily, the Army's example demonstrates that significant progress can be made

---

[44] Moskos and Butler 66-67.

through intentional effort and commitment. The Christian Church has access to resources that the Army does not have. Through the Word and the Spirit, we should be able to replace ethnocentrism and oppression with justice and shalom.

Tainting Our Afterlife

Each of us has someone
We know we really ought to love
But that other is so utterly foreign
So fundamentally different
So completely wrong about nearly everything
That the thought of them
Tainting our afterlife
Is almost more than we can bear…

…Until we recall
That the chasm Christ bridged
Between a holy God
And our wholly fallen souls
Was infinitely wider
Than the gulf between us and those
Who show forth an equally—
Just differently—
Distorted image of the Redeemer
Who bought the two
For one prohibitive price

Chapter Three

Rich and Poor

black brothers and sisters perishing
on a lonely island of poverty
in the midst of a
vast ocean of material prosperity
Dr. Martin Luther King, Jr.

Blessed are the poor
Woe to the rich
Luke 6:20 & 24

The Poor

Who are the poor? Put simply, the poor are people who lack the necessities of life – things such as clean water, nutritious food, decent shelter, access to health care, education, etc. The poor are seldom arrogant; life has humbled them. They are more apt to be poor in spirit, to acknowledge their need of help, of God, unless their poverty and oppression has crushed them to the point that they cannot do this (see previous chapter). Some oppressed poor are broken in body, mind and spirit.

But a warning at this point. Just by putting a label on them, it is exceedingly easy for any of us to categorize the poor, to stereotype them. Even for those of us who, following the Scriptures, want to "help" them. The poor are persons created in the image of God. They have dignity, which must be respected and guarded.

The following is a true story. I heard this from the lips of the woman who experienced the following as an "Okie" migrant child.

During the Great Depression and Dust Bowl era of the 1930s, many citizens fled Oklahoma to try and make a living elsewhere. A teacher noticed that "Jane" was malnourished, so she discreetly arranged for Jane to go into the teacher's lounge and pour herself a glass of milk each day. The teacher eventually found out that Jane was pouring her daily glass of milk down the drain. She could not accept even well-meaning charity.

Another teacher noticed that Jane needed glasses. She took Jane to her own eye doctor and arranged for glasses. When the glasses were delivered, Jane refused to accept them. Then the teacher told Jane a story. When the teacher was a little girl, someone gave *her* a pair of glasses. Now she was doing the same thing. Jane accepted the glasses. No longer was she a recipient of charity; instead, she was a trusted courier who someday could bless someone else in need.

As a person reads the full gospel of Luke, one is struck by the many negative passages about the rich, money, greed, etc. The poor have many problems and needs; thus Jesus spends much of his time among them, ministering to their needs. But Jesus never identifies the poor as *the* social problem, as we commonly do in America today. Instead the rich are castigated as *the* social problem. This point is concisely captured in the phrase: "Woe to the rich..." (6:24), which sums up Luke's attitude toward the rich.

We cannot understand who the poor are and why they are poor just by studying the poor and identifying their characteristics. The rich and poor are not isolated from each other, even though the rich or society may try to segregate the poor into a ghetto. Rather, they stand in relationship to each other in society. Tax breaks for the rich discriminate against the poor. "Good news to the poor" ministries must understand and deal with this dynamic.

So again, the poor are people, created in the image of God. They are precious in His sight. So much so that one of the important factors on judgment day will be how we treated the poor (Mt. 25:31-46). Those who fed the hungry, gave the thirsty a drink, etc., were called blessed. Those who did not minister to the poor and needy were cursed and sent to eternal punishment.

A similar point is made in Proverbs 14:31: "He who oppresses the poor shows contempt for their Maker, but whoever is kind to the needy honors God."

The NIV concordance lists 176 references to the poor, 134 in the Old Testament and 42 in the New Testament. There are 15 references to poverty in the Old Testament and five in the New Testament. Poverty is more than an ideological issue to be debated; the poor are a theological issue because though they are created in the image of God, they are too often crushed and dehumanized.

According to Lawrence Richards, author of *Expository Dictionary of Bible Words*, the words translated as "poor" in the Old Testament most commonly refer to real material poverty, and only occasionally to spiritual poverty.[45] *Dal* refers to the lower class; *ani* refers to the "pain of the oppressed poor...the socially powerless..." *Ebyon* "connotes a person in dire want," the economically needy and socially dependent. The poor are vulnerable, powerless, and easily exploited by a ruthless person in power and authority.

In the New Testament, the primary word for poor, *ptochos*, occurs 34 times, and it carries much the same meaning as the Old Testament words for the poor. Richards says that *ptochos* refers to "those reduced almost to a beggarly situation." A less common word, *penes*, refers to the person without property who had to work for a low wage, in many cases, a day laborer. Income would have been minimal, uncertain and subject to exploitation (James 5:4).

In summary, the poor of the Bible are usually deprived, destitute, dependent or "dirt poor." Jacques Ellul, in his brilliant book, *Money and Power*, concludes that "without money, people are only paupers. They stand outside society and have hardly any place or function...when they have nothing, they do not exist."[46] But in God's eyes, the poor are of great value.

---

[45] Lawrence Richards, *Expository Dictionary of Bible Words* (Grand Rapids, MI: Zondervan, 1991).
[46] Jacques Ellul, *Money and Power* (Downers Grove, IL: Inter-Varsity Press, 1984) 21.

Why are the poor poor? Before we proceed, I should warn you that this can be a hazardous question to ask. Bishop Camara of Brazil once said, "When I feed the poor, they call me a saint. When I ask why the poor are poor, they call me a communist."

According to the Scriptures, the causes of poverty are multiple. Sometimes poverty is created by natural disasters such as drought, floods, hurricanes or earthquakes. Many proverbs indicate that laziness is a cause of some poverty. For instance, "Lazy hands make a man poor..." (10:4). The New Testament echoes this sentiment: "If a man will not work, he shall not eat" (II Thess. 3:10).

But the most common cause of poverty, according to the Bible, is oppression, injustice. The prophets and, surprisingly, the psalmists highlight oppression as a cause of poverty, and the Proverbs also support this cause (see 13:23 and 14:31).

In summary, the poor are persons created in the image of God. Most commonly, the poor are crushed, dehumanized, oppressed persons who struggle to maintain their dignity as human beings. This is why God is so often pictured as deeply concerned about the plight of the poor person. As followers of God, we should be deeply concerned as well.

The Rich

The rich are also persons created in the image of God. Sometimes in the Scriptures, especially in the Old Testament, wealthy people, such as Abraham and Job, are presented as humble individuals who were blessed by God. Some rich people handle their wealth wisely and give generously.

Tragically, however, most of the rich in the Bible trade their God-like image for a mess of pottage. Riches become Mammon, their god; too often, the rich become idolaters and oppressors. Jacques Ellul states, "From one end of the Bible to the other rings out a curse on the rich," and "judgment against the rich is always radical," because the "accumulation of money is always linked with sin, whether at the beginning or as a consequence."[47]

In the Old Testament, there are 57 references to rich and 34 to riches. In the New Testament, there are 41 references to rich and 17 to riches. There are a total of 149 references to the rich and riches, and 176 references to the poor. There are 128 references to oppression, most often in the context of the rich oppressing the poor. There are in fact many more references to the rich and the poor than a specific word count indicates. For example, Amos 3:15 obviously refers to the rich (i.e., the inhabitants of mansions) even though the specific word is not used. These large numbers obviously indicate that the rich and riches are important Biblical themes.

Lawrence Richards brilliantly presents the two Old Testament perspectives on wealth. The person, the nation, that obeys God, that keeps the covenant relationship with God, will be blessed by God as is indicated in Psalm 112:3: "Wealth and riches are in his house, and his righteousness endures forever." Richards asserts that by "Jesus' time this theme had been interpreted to imply that riches were a clear sign of God's favor. A person who was rich was *ipso facto* righteous, one of God's blessed ones."[48] If this is true, the Pharisees were highly blessed, for they were lovers of money.

Because of the pervasiveness of human sin, riches can become a dangerous perversion, so the Old Testament warns again and again against trusting in riches. Amos, for example, thunders against the misuse of riches (2:6-7):

> They sell the righteous for silver
>> and the needy for a pair of sandals.
> They trample on the heads of the poor...
>> and deny justice to the oppressed.

---

[47] Ellul 10.
[48] Richards, see article on "Rich."

Not only will God destroy idolatrous altars, but he will also destroy the idolatrous houses of the rich (3:15):

> I will tear down the winter house
>> along with the summer house;
> the houses adorned with ivory will be destroyed
>> and the mansions will be demolished.

Judgment will fall upon the rich "women who oppress the poor and crush the needy" (4:11). Amos 5:11-12: "You trample on the poor...you oppress the righteous and you deprive the poor of justice in the courts."

In the New Testament, there is an overwhelming bias against the rich. Rarely do you find passages that assert that riches are a blessing from God. The basic attitude of the New Testament is found in Luke 6: 20 and 24: "Blessed are you who are poor... Woe to you who are rich..." The same spirit is reflected in Luke 16:13-14: "'...you cannot serve both God and Money.' The Pharisees, who loved money, heard all of this and were sneering at Jesus."

In conclusion, poverty is a desperate state for any human being to be in, since this person lacks the necessities of life. On the other hand, riches are a dangerous state to be in, because they are an enormous temptation for one to become self-sufficient and forget God. Proverbs 30:8-9 states the issue well:

> Give me neither poverty nor riches,
>> but give me only my daily bread.
> Otherwise, I may have too much and disown you
>> and say, "Who is the Lord?"
> Or I may become poor and steal,
>> and so dishonor the name of my God.

A Sociotheology of Riches and Poverty

Some Christians claim that riches are value-neutral, that the problem is not money, but the love of money. They may cite

Paul's statement that "the love of money is a root of all kinds of evil" (I Tim. 6:10). While there is some truth to the assertion that it is our attitude toward money that is crucial, the personal attitude approach does not resolve all the problems associated with riches and poverty.

Rich people possess more than the necessities of life; they can enjoy the luxuries of life as well. They usually control an undue portion of property, land and resources. Poor people lack the necessities of life; they usually own little or no property, land or resources. Therefore, they lack control of their own economic destiny.

The above hints at a crucial element in developing a sociotheology of riches and poverty. The rich person and the poor person coexist in relationship in a community or society. Riches and poverty are not unrelated phenomena which can be studied in isolation from each other.

Can shalom exist in a community if one person is rich, and another person is poor? Shalom is a state of well-being in every area of life – spiritual, social, economic and physical. It is obvious that a poor person lacks shalom, but so does the rich person. Shalom is a state of blessing from God shared in community. The rich person experiences comfort and a measure of peace, but that is a superficial shalom. Shalom calls for poverty to cease. What is the role of the rich in the achievement of shalom? Generosity and justice?

Often in the Old Testament, and almost always in the New Testament, riches or the rich person are condemned. Why? In the Old Testament, the prophets railed against the rich and powerful because the rich gained their riches by oppressing the poor. They might seize the poor person's land in an unethical and illegal fashion or pay low wages. Not only would such economic oppression leave a person without the necessities of life, but it would crush, humiliate, and animalize the poor person who is equally created in the image of God. **Certainly oppression and shalom cannot coexist in a healthy community.**

The solution to the rich-poor problem is doing justice (fair and just socioeconomic judgments from the leaders of a society), so that oppression is stopped and the standard of righteousness is restored in community relationships. Love and charity will always be needed, but charity alone leaves the poor person dependent on the rich for a handout. Charity alone provides a superficial shalom. Full shalom demands that justice be done, that oppression cease.

The problem with riches, according to the New Testament, is much more serious than most Christians realize. Apparently, for most rich persons, riches are a form of idolatry. "No immoral, impure or greedy person – such a man is an idolater – has any inheritance in the kingdom of Christ and of God" (Eph. 5:5).

The idolatry of riches has serious social consequences. It leads to an environment where wealth and property become more important than persons. The idolatry of riches affects one's personal attitudes and values. The inner motivation of love is replaced by greed, covetousness. "People who want to get rich fall into temptation and a trap and into many foolish and harmful desires that plunge men into ruin and destruction… Some people, eager for money, have wandered from the faith and pierced themselves with many griefs" (I Tim. 6:9-10).

Paul makes riches sound dangerous; he indicates that they can lead to bondage, and, in a sense, become addicting. It may be that, in reality, riches are more addictive than are alcohol and crack cocaine. Why is it, then, that so many of us rationalize the legitimacy of riches, that so many of us would willingly take the risk of being rich? We tend to think that I would be the exception, that I could be rich and not become idolatrous, that I could be rich and not oppress people in the process, that I could be rich and not become covetous, that I could be rich and not succumb to the addictiveness of riches. Sorry, Christian friend, according to Jesus Christ and Paul, the odds are not in your favor.

What happens when the rich are fully converted? When Zacchaeus, the rich tax collector, met Jesus, he repented and engaged in restitution. "Here and now I give half my possessions to the poor, and if I have cheated anybody out of anything, I will pay back four times the amount" (Luke 19:8). Acts 4:32-35 describes a church in which the rich share so generously that there were no poor in the church. Incredible!

We must beware lest American cultural values regarding the rich and poor lead us to reject the radical Scriptural teaching on this topic. Only if we use the Biblical concepts of oppression, justice and shalom to develop a sociotheology of rich and poor will we avoid allowing the American trinity of individualism, materialism and racism to inform our perspective on riches and poverty.

In summary, the problem with riches is:

social   1) getting them wrongly – oppression

personal   2) the individual's attitude – greed, covetousness

spiritual   3) their exaggerated importance – idolatry

bondage   4) their addictive properties – always wanting ("needing") more

The Religious Rich According to Luke

In New Testament times, a rich religio-politico-economic elite ran Jewish society. Therefore, the themes of the rich, riches, greed, etc. become very important in Luke. Note the following passages from his gospel account:

Luke 4:18-19   The Spirit of the Lord is on me,
because he has anointed me
to preach good news to the poor...
to release the oppressed,
to proclaim Jubilee justice for the poor.
(Noble paraphrase)

Luke 6: 20,24   Blessed are you who are poor...
Woe to you who are rich...

Luke 11:39-42   Pharisees...you are full of greed and wickedness...you neglect justice and the love of God.

Luke 18:22-24   Sell everything you have and give it to the poor...When he heard this, he became very sad, because he was a man of great wealth...How hard it is for the rich to enter the kingdom of God.

Luke 19:45-46   Then he entered the temple area and began driving out those who were selling... you have made my house a den of robbers.

Luke19:8   Here and now I give half of my possessions to the poor.

See also Luke 1:53; 3:10-14; 8:14; 12:13-34.

The Rich-Poor Gap: From Bad to Worse

The American poor are poor in two ways: income-poor and asset-poor. Approximately 25 percent of Afro Americans are income-poor; around 50 percent are asset-poor or wealth-poor.

In the October 2, 2006, issue of *U.S. News and World Report*, editor-in-chief Mortimer Zuckerman summarizes and interprets the income gap in an editorial entitled, "For a Fairer America." *U.S. News* is the most conservative of the three major weekly news magazines. Zuckerman states:

> The income gap between the richest and poorest Americans is wider than at any time in history, and we must take urgent measures to begin closing it.[49]

---

[49] Mortimer Zuckerman, "For a Fairer America," *U.S. News and World Report* 2 Oct. 2006: 79.

We live in a new "Gilded Age." In 1873, Mark Twain coined the phrase in a satire to describe the shameless rich who flaunted their massive wealth. Zuckerman's description of the first Gilded Age: "The country worshipped gold, its politics were venal, and 1 percent of Americans sat on 20 percent of the nation's wealth."

After the Great Depression, after World War II:

> ...income growth soared, thanks to the happy confluence of private enterprise and government benefits. Social Security and Medicare freed families from worries about providing for their elderly parents, while the GI bill and student loans enlarged the middle class. **Income inequality**, as a consequence, **shrank sharply** through the 1970s in a phenomenon called the "Great Compression." (emphasis added)

Today, however, Zuckerman asserts:

> The wealth escalator doesn't work... Since the 1970s, **inequality** of income and wealth has **increased dramatically**.[50] (emphasis added)

Unrestrained capitalism, though enormously productive, generates this rich-poor gap, so Zuckerman proposes three government measures to bring a degree of economic justice to America:

* More support for education at all levels;
* A major effort to brake soaring health care costs; and
* A new minimum wage.

Kevin Phillips, a secular prophet, is also deeply worried about our rich-poor gap, our wealth gap; he sees it as a threat to

---

[50] Ibid.

American democracy. In his book, *Wealth and Democracy*, Phillips states:

> In searching for what was common to twenty-one past civilizations that had failed, the historian Arnold J. Toynbee identified 'concentrated ownership.'[51]

In short, concentrated ownership of land and resources was unjust and led to pride, greed, arrogance and corruption.

The early church fathers were also concerned about concentrated ownership. Augustine considered it legitimate to own a plot of land in order to be self-sufficient, but he was fiercely opposed to the Roman idea of private property without restrictions. The Roman policy allowed a few rich people to accumulate wealth and property in an unlimited fashion. For more on this, see Chapter Five for a discussion of Charles Avila's *Ownership: Early Christian Teaching*. Augustine's position was consistent with the teaching of the Old Testament Jubilee, which promoted household ownership of land, but broke up patterns of concentrated ownership every 50 years.

Back to American history. According to Kevin Phillips:

> Many of the declaration's [Declaration of Independence] signers were representatives of America's richest families... Theirs was a *revolutionary* document with respect to Britain, but not in matters domestic... Hierarchy [class divisions, rich over poor, an elite] was a fact of life in the eighteenth-century American colonies.[52]

There was an attempt to add a sixteenth article to the Bill of Rights which would have restricted concentrated ownership. This article was defeated. This is how it was stated:

---

[51] Kevin Phillips, *Wealth and Democracy: A Political History of the American Rich,* (Broadway Books, 2003) 373.

[52] Phillips, *Wealth and Democracy*, 5.

An Enormous Proportion of Property vested in a few individuals is dangerous to the rights, and Destructive of the Common Happiness of Mankind, and therefore, every free State hath a right by its laws to discourage the Possession of Such Property.[53]

Our founding fathers were a white, male, propertied (i.e., rich) elite who benefited from concentrated ownership, so this article was defeated. This valuing of the rich over the poor has haunted American history down to the present day. During the colonial period, wars made many Americans rich, piracy made many rich, government contracts made many rich, and corruption made many rich. Much the same thing happened during the Civil War.

In response to the excessive wealth and abuse of the Gilded Age, some reform in American democracy occurred during the T. Roosevelt, Wilson, and F.D.R. eras. But in the 1980s, President Reagan re-opened the door to massive wealth accumulation. Reagan said, "What I want to see above all is that this remains a country where someone can always get rich." Phillips documents that this wish became fact:

Between 1979 and 1989 the portion of the nation's wealth held by the top 1 percent nearly doubled, skyrocketing from 22 percent to 39 percent, probably the most rapid [wealth] escalation in U.S. history.[54]

President George W. Bush continued the Reagan legacy; he is very compassionate to the rich. Does this violate the standards of Biblical justice? If John the Baptist were present, he would call for repentance. See Luke 3:7-11:

You brood of vipers... Produce fruit in keeping with repentance... Anyone who has two shirts should share with

---

[53] Phillips, *Wealth and Democracy*, 6.
[54] Phillips, *Wealth and Democracy*, 92.

the one who has none, and anyone who has food should do the same. (TNIV)

But instead of repenting and sharing, the new American gospel promotes rejoicing and piling. The front cover of the September 18, 2006, issue of *Time* magazine pictures an up-close shot of a Rolls Royce grill with a small metal cross perched on top of the grill. The headline on the front cover reads: "Does **God** want you to be **Rich?**"[55] Inside the magazine we find a familiar Scripture reinterpreted, "Why **not gain** the whole world **plus** my soul?" The prosperity gospel has become so rampant that the secular *Time* magazine highlights it as a national concern.

The snake in our midst has been sanctified!

---

[55] David Biema and Jeff Chu, "Does God Want You To Be Rich?" *Time* 18 Sep. 2006: 48-56.

Amos 3:15 (reprised)

The mansions sit atop the hills
    Ornate
    Aloof
    Secure

Untouchable by anyone
not deemed worthy to approach
unless they come to cook
    or clean
    or tutor
    or mow

But then God breathes
And the winds come
    with the rains
    and the mud
    or the fire

And the idols cower
in inanimate impotence
before falling
    or flooding
    or sliding
    or burning

Until nothing remains
but a slab
and a choice

Chapter Four

Oppression and Oppressors

Oppression in a society can become so rampant that its
elimination, by whatever means are necessary, becomes an
all-consuming end for many people. To this day, ideologies of
revolution originate in that experience. They belong to a type of
ideology aimed at spearheading or inciting radical societal
change. The ideology of the French Revolution was born as a
response to horrific exploitation, carried out under the existing
empire of clergy and nobility. Oppression in the French countryside, particularly by the landed nobility, was so severe that
children died like rats... **Most church leaders...shrouded this
oppression in resounding silence.**[56] (emphasis added)
Bob Goudzwaard, Awakening Hope

B iblically, the church should always be on the forefront of
ministry among the poor and oppressed. If this were a
common pattern, there would be no need for radical ideologies
to spring up to champion the cause of the oppressed.

Currently the wealth gap between Euro Americans and Afro
Americans is 10-1, and we've seen how this present inequity is
closely connected to a past characterized by severe oppression.
**Why is the white evangelical church silent about this horren-
dous evil?**

---

[56] Bob Goudzwaard, et al., *Awakening Hope: Unmasking the
Idols of our Times,* (pre-publication manuscript, 2006) 39.

Oppression and Shalom

First, a look at oppression and shalom in the Old Testament.

> The Lord said to Moses, "Tell Aaron and his sons, 'This is
> how you are to bless the Israelites. Say to them:
> "The Lord bless you
> and keep you;
> the Lord make his face shine upon you
> and be gracious to you;
> the Lord turn his face toward you
> and give you peace [shalom]"'" (Numbers 6:22-26).

Here the blessing of God is the grace of God resting upon his obedient people and granting them shalom. Shalom is a rich word meaning more than peace; it carries a sense of wholeness, completeness, harmony. Shalom is a total sense of well-being not only for individuals but also for a community, a people walking with God together. The blessing of shalom supports well-being in every area of life – spiritual, social, economic and physical. The people blessed with shalom experienced joy in life.

It is rather obvious why a true prophet of God would preach and promote shalom. But the false prophets also proclaimed shalom, according to Jeremiah. Jeremiah 6:14 and 8:11 state: "They have healed the wound of my people lightly, saying 'Peace, peace,' when there is no peace." Or "'Shalom, shalom,' when there is no shalom."

If there was no peace, no shalom, what was there? Again and again, the prophet thundered that there was religious idolatry and social oppression. In Jeremiah 6:13 and 8:10, we hear oppression described: "Because from the least to the greatest, everyone is greedy for unjust gain; from prophet to priest everyone deals falsely."

Or Jeremiah 5:26-28:

> For wicked men are found among my people... Therefore
> they have become great and rich, they have grown fat and

sleek. They know no bounds in deeds of wickedness; they judge not with justice the cause of the fatherless, to make it prosper, and they do not defend the rights of the needy.

In talking about Jerusalem, the key city in Israel, Jeremiah declares: "This is the city which must be punished; there is nothing but oppression within her" (6:6). Jeremiah 7:6 calls on Israel not to "oppress the alien, the fatherless or the widow... " Or Jeremiah 9:6: "'Heaping oppression upon oppression, and deceit upon deceit, they refuse to know me,' says the Lord."

Oppression, then, is the opposite of shalom and the absence of justice. Oppression and shalom are polar opposites. Oppression may be the most horrible word in human language; shalom may be the most beautiful. I am a little leery of some of the shalom theology that is out there; it may be "shalom lite" if it first does not take a hard look at oppression. What is oppression? It is the cruel and unjust exercise of power and authority, usually through social institutions. What does oppression do to people? **It crushes, humiliates, animalizes, impoverishes, enslaves and kills people created in the image of God.**[57]

In contrast, shalom occurs when a community, a people of God, walks in covenant with God and fellow human beings according to the standards of justice and righteousness. Oppression crushes people; justice/shalom releases the crushed ones. Oppression humiliates persons; justice/shalom affirms persons. Oppression animalizes people; justice/shalom humanizes people. Oppression impoverishes people; justice/shalom prospers (necessities of life) people. Oppression kills persons; only justice beyond this life can provide shalom for these persons.

Until the 1980s, there was relatively little scholarly analysis of the Biblical concept of oppression, especially in English and

---

[57] Thomas Hanks, *God So Loved the Third World: The Biblical Vocabulary of Oppression* (Maryknoll, NY: Orbis Books, 1983) 38+.

written by evangelicals, including in standard Bible dictionaries and encyclopedias. The only thorough article that I know of on oppression is found in the revised *International Standard Bible Encyclopedia*, with a total of 222 lines[58]; the 1929 *ISBE* had a brief article of 30 lines. The 1986 *ISBE* article on oppression draws heavily on research done by Thomas Hanks and Elsa Tamez, who taught in Costa Rica.

The norm, however, is no listing of oppression, as in *The Illustrated Bible Dictionary* (1980) published by InterVarsity Press; this dictionary lists oracle, orchard and ordination, but not oppression, in spite of the fact that there are approximately 128 occurrences of the word oppression in the NIV translation.

A question: Why this lack of scholarly interest in and research about the important concept of oppression? Have our theologians come primarily from the middle and upper classes? Do they lack exposure and/or sensitivity to the experience of oppression? Even today, among North American evangelicals, there is little scholarship on oppression. No Christian book on poverty that I have read includes a chapter on oppression.

In 1983, Thomas Hanks, a North American evangelical teaching at the Latin American Biblical Seminary in Costa Rica, published the English-language version of his book (originally written in Spanish), *God So Loved The Third World: The Biblical Vocabulary of Oppression*. One year earlier, the English translation of Elsa Tamez's *Bible of the Oppressed* had appeared. Tamez is a Mexican evangelical colleague of Hanks.

Tamez states that "there is an almost complete absence of the theme of oppression in European and North American Biblical theology." [59] Hanks asserts:

---

[58] *International Standard Bible Encyclopedia*, ed. Geoffrey W. Bromiley (Grand Rapids, MI: Wm. B. Eerdmans Publishing Company, 1986) 609-611.

[59] Elsa Tamez, *Bible of the Oppressed* (Maryknoll, NY: Orbis Books, 1982) 4.

Anyone who has read much in the theological classics (Augustine, Luther, Calvin, Barth, Berkouwer et al.) will recognize that the theme of oppression has received little or no attention there. One might think that the Bible says little about oppression. Furthermore, one searches in vain for the theme in Bible dictionaries, encyclopedias, and the like.

However, when we strike the rock of a complete Bible concordance, to our great surprise we hit a gusher of texts and terms that deal with oppression! In short, we find a **basic structural category of Biblical theology.**

After a thorough study of Hebrew roots for oppression, Hanks concludes:

> **Oppression is a fundamental structural category of Biblical theology**, as is evidenced by the large number of Hebrew roots denoting it (10 basic roots; 20 in all); the frequency of their occurrence (555 times); the basic theological character of many texts that speak of it (Gen. 15; Exod. 1-5; Ps. 72, 103, 146; Isa. 8-9, 42, 53, 58, etc.); and the significance of oppression in Israel's great creedal confession (Deut. 26:5-9).[60]

In my judgment, unless a person has a profound understanding of the **horror of oppression,** one is unlikely to develop a **passionate, wise concern** for **social justice.** By and large, the church has not had a Biblical understanding of oppression; and by and large, the church has done little to execute justice on behalf of the fatherless, the alien and the widow. Some charity, yes; some reform, yes; but little fundamental social justice. This approach allows white evangelicals to maintain white privilege while doing some good and salving their consciences.

Perry Yoder, an Old Testament scholar and author of *Shalom*, says that the major thesis of his book is that shalom "is squarely against injustice and oppression. Indeed, we shall ar-

---

[60] Hanks 38.

gue that shalom demands a transforming of unjust social and economic orders."[61] In order to achieve shalom, we must "do justice," "execute justice," "pursue justice," and "give justice." Justice must be active and aggressive. Note Psalm 82:3-4: "Give justice to the weak and fatherless; maintain the rights of the afflicted and the destitute. Rescue the weak and needy; deliver them from the hand of the wicked."

In summary, oppression and shalom are polar opposites. Justice stands in the middle, and it is two-pronged. On one side, it releases, liberates the oppressed; on the other, it provides access to the resources of God's creation so a family can be self-sufficient.

The Temple: A System of Oppression

Now a look at oppression in operation in the New Testament. I wish to illustrate how the Biblical concepts – the cosmos (evil social order), the powers and authorities, oppression and ethnocentrism – are incarnated in the cultural values and the operation of the Temple at the time of Christ. While there are no passages of Scripture which specifically describe the functioning of the temple in the way I am about to do, I think the concepts I will be using are Scripturally based and can be logically applied to the temple.

Jesus, as he was teaching in the temple area, told the Jewish leaders, "You belong to your father, the devil" (John 8:44). I conclude that Satan, working through the fallen powers and authorities, had essentially gained control of the temple. The temple had become an evil social institution used to oppress and exploit the people for the benefit of the Jewish religio-politico-economic elite. The members of this elite class were using their religious power and authority base to become rich. Sincere individual Jewish worshippers might still come to the temple and

---

[61] Perry Yoder, *Shalom* (Newton, KS: Faith and Life Press, 1987) 5.

offer acceptable sacrifices to God, but the leadership had become thoroughly corrupt.

The high priests, as the leaders of Israel, and the temple, as the most important social institution, were the center of the Jewish social order. Listen to this concise description of the Jewish evil social order given by Juan Mateos in the introduction to a Spanish edition of the New Testament. Mateos is a Jesuit scholar in Biblical studies; the following quotation is from a 1977 issue of *Sojourners* magazine:

> The high priests were the official representatives of religion and worship who had charge of the temple. All Jews over twelve years of age, including those who had lived abroad (and they were many), had to pay an annual temple tax equivalent to two days' work (Matthew 17:24). For the maintenance of the clergy they also had to pay ten percent of the harvest (Matthew 23:23). Besides this, the temple received gifts (Mark 7:11) and abundant alms, above all from the rich (Mk. 12:41), not to mention the livestock market for the sacrifices and the currency exchange (Mk. 11:15). All this turned the temple into a great commercial racket administered by the high priests. They represented the political and religious power, and were at the same time an important financial group to be reckoned with.[62]

The chosen people had become a corrupt people; in my opinion, at least as corrupt as Israel was at the time of the Old Testament prophets. Israel was characterized as idolatrous, oppressive and immoral. The prophets declared, "do justice or face judgment."

"Church" and "state" were not separate institutions in New Testament Judaism. Neither was the economic system separate. The religious leaders controlled it all in one nice, neat package, giving them unprecedented power, and this power corrupted. The temple was a powerful economic institution. A French

---

[62] Juan Mateos, "The Message of Jesus," *Sojourners* July 1977: 9.

scholar described it this way: It combined the functions of the U.S. Treasury, the Federal Reserve System and Wall Street together. This might be an exaggeration, but it makes a powerful point. Mateos continues:

> The city of Jerusalem was practically supported by the large temple revenues, especially at seasons of pilgrimage – three times a year – when besides the Palestinians came Jews from the diaspora and foreigners as well (John 12:30). The second group in the Council was made up of Senators (elders) who were laymen chosen from among the aristocratic families. For the most part they were the great landowners and were the backbone of the Sadducee Party, to which the high priests belonged... The Pharisees had immense authority over the people... In spite of all their observations of religious rules, the Pharisees loved money and exploited the simple folk under the pretext of piety (Mt. 23:25-28; Mk. 12:40; Luke 1:39, 16:14).[63]

Donald Kraybill's *The Upside-Down Kingdom*, chapters three and four, provides the following information about the city of Jerusalem, the temple and the wealth and power of the Jewish leaders. First, some comments about the holy city of Jerusalem:

> We have seen the spectacular beauty of Jerusalem as Judaism's highest religious peak. It also towered above the rest of the country in social and economic prestige. An elite aristocracy called Jerusalem their home. This included the chief priests of the temple hierarchy, wealthy landowners, merchants, tax collectors, and the Sadducean Party. Men of wealth who could live off the rent from their estates, skilled artists, clever traders, and poets all migrated toward the metropolis which housed the temple. Jerusalem wasn't

---

[63] Mateos 10.

merely the foremost of Judean cities; there actually were no second- or third-rate ones.

Extravagance oozed from the affluent elite. They wrapped gold bindings around the palm branches which they carried to festive temple ceremonies. They brought their offering of first fruits in golden vessels on Pentecost...

Many of the rich in Jerusalem derived their wealth from vast estates in the country.[64]

Because many peasant farmers were forced to mortgage their property to pay high Roman and Jewish taxes, these farmers were losing the land. Many of the properties became temple property. Kraybill comments:

"Within a few decades, small and middle-sized plots of land had disappeared, whereas the properties owned by the temple and the imperial crown grew beyond proportion... Driven to misery, many peasants abandoned their land and joined bands of robbers that survived by pillage and lived in caves in the mountains." (quoted from Andre Trocme)

At the core of the poverty was a system of double taxation which was overbearing to the poor peasant. First, two dozen or so different types of Jewish tithes and offerings were required of the devout Jew. On top of this religious system were the numerous taxes which the Romans extracted. Although it is difficult to calculate the exact proportion of taxes, most scholars agree that forty to seventy percent of the peasant's annual income eventually fell into the hands of various kinds of tax collectors and creditors.[65]

---

[64] Donald Kraybill, *The Upside-Down Kingdom* (Scottdale, PA: Herald Press, 1978) 82.
[65] Kraybill 86.

The temple was the center of religious life for the 500,000 Jews living in Palestine and the three and one-half million Jews in the Roman Empire. (This is Kraybill's estimate; the *ISBE* estimates three million in Palestine and four million in the Dispersion.) The temple was huge, covering 26 acres. It was magnificent; the gold and silver made it look like a snowcapped peak from the nearby countryside. "There was so much gold in the temple that after its destruction and plunder in AD 70, the province of Syria was glutted with gold reducing its value by half."[66]

In conclusion, Kraybill states:

> The political, social, and religious affairs of all Judea and international Judaism were oriented toward the great temple in Jerusalem. Synagogues in each village throughout the countryside faced the holy temple. The temple's influence permeated the hinterland through the network of 18,000 priests and Levites whose social and religious status was tied into the temple operation. The frequent pilgrimages and trips for sacrifice cemented even the ordinary Jewish peasant into the temple's mystique.[67]

When Jesus cleansed the temple, he called it a "den of robbers" or "a cave of social bandits" or, my paraphrase, "a religiously legitimated system of oppression." How was the ordinary, poor peasant exploited by the operation of the temple? William Barclay (in his book, *By What Authority?*) describes in some detail the type of religious exploitation that occurred. Temple taxes could not be paid with coins with a head engraved on the coin – a graven image. So the religious pilgrim would have to have the coin exchanged for a shekel without a head on it. They would usually be charged an exorbitant fee for this service.

The same thing happened with animal sacrifices. Outside the temple, a pigeon could be purchased for five new pence. In-

---

[66] Kraybill 66.
[67] Kraybill 71.

side the temple, a pigeon might cost 75 new pence. Temple inspectors often required pilgrims to purchase sacrifices inside the temple to be sure the sacrifice was without a blemish.

Barclay explains:

> Three things infuriated Jesus about this. First, the whole business was a ramp [racket] in which pilgrims were being ruthlessly fleeced. Jesus' action was first of all a blow for social justice. Second, the huckstering and the bargaining and the arguing must have made the place a pandemonium in which any kind of prayer or meditation or worship was quite impossible. Third, the whole business was taking place in the Court of the Gentiles, the only part of the Temple into which a Gentile might come... This action of Jesus was a blow for social justice, a scathing rebuke of irreverence, a defense of the rights of Gentiles... That was the most astonishing display of authority that Jesus ever enacted.[68]

Let us now turn to Luke's description of the cleansing of the temple, a rather mild phrase to describe what really happened (19:45-46):

> Then he entered the temple area and began driving out those who were selling. "It is written," he said to them, "'My house will be a house of prayer,' but you have made it 'a den of robbers.'"

In Luke, the chief priests come on the scene for the first time as Jesus challenges their power and authority. They pointedly ask Jesus: "Tell us by what authority you are doing these things." Then, in the temple itself, Jesus tells a parable directed against them (see Luke 20:1-19). Not only in the physical cleansing of the temple, but also in his teaching in the temple, Jesus directly challenged the leadership of the temple.

---

[68] Barclay 96.

Jesus, in effect, took over the temple for a few days. In another deceptively mild statement, Luke's first sentence following the cleansing is, "Every day he was teaching at the temple... all the people hung on his words" (Luke 19:47-48).

The chief priests stood helplessly by in a rage, plotting to kill Jesus, as Jesus took over "their" temple and taught against them and taught the kingdom of God (21:31). Two whole chapters document the radical nature of Jesus' teaching in the temple. This section closes with another mild understatement considering the enormous significance of these events:

> Each day Jesus was teaching at the temple... and all the people came early in the morning to hear him at the temple (21:37-8).

In Matthew, it is likely that most, if not all, of chapters 21:12 through 23:39 took place in or near the temple. Apparently, the seven woes directed against the teachers of the law and the Pharisees were issued from inside the temple. Jesus used the strongest possible words to condemn the whole corrupt religious system and, especially, the leaders of that system. **Jesus hated the misuse of God as a cover for ethnocentrism and oppression.**

What are some lessons to be learned from the temple confrontation initiated by Jesus?

1. Social evil in social institutions is deeply ingrained, often legitimated by religion, and therefore highly resistant to change.

2. In order to bring about social change, social conflict must be initiated. The social evil and the evil leaders must be aggressively and publicly exposed.

3. At the same time that one exposes social evil, one must present a positive alternative – the kingdom of God social order characterized by socioeconomic justice.

4. In this process, the common people must be central. Remember that as Jesus taught in the temple "all the people hung on his words." Prior to this, the chief priests and the teachers of the law were the leaders of the people, using religion to manipulate the people (19:47). The chief priests wanted to kill Jesus immediately, but they did not dare to, because of the power of the people (19:48; 20:19; 22:2). Luke refers to "the people" a number of times in this section (19:47-8; 20:1, 9, 16, 45; 22:37-8).

5. Great care must be used in identifying the central social evil in society. What most people, including (or especially) the leaders, identify as the main social evil may, in fact, not be the real problem. It may be a smokescreen to divert attention from the really important social evil.

Note that Jesus did not target the Roman headquarters in Palestine or identify Rome as the social evil; for most Jews of the day, Roman domination was the social evil. Though Rome was oppressive in its imperialistic rule of Palestine, Jesus never initiated an anti-Roman campaign. Rome is barely mentioned in the gospels. Jesus was shrewd enough to realize where the heart of the problem was located. Even if the Roman occupation had miraculously ceased overnight, the Jewish religio-politico-economic elite would have continued to oppress the people.

Politicians and others who benefit from an internal system of oppression will often focus on an outside system of oppression as the great social evil to fight against. Unless Christians are Biblically wise and sensitive to the leading of the Holy Spirit, they, too, can be misled and manipulated by clever ideological propaganda. Beware of anti-_____ (fill-in-the-blank) campaigns which focus on "them" as the bad guys and "us" as the good guys. Read *The Wars of America: Christian Views,* in which eight

Christian historians analyze why we really fought our wars, and how most Christians bought into the ideological propaganda used to justify these wars.[69]

Oppression: Biblical and Experiential

I said before that unless a person grasps the **horror of oppression,** one is unlikely to develop a **passion for justice.** So how can a person who has not experienced oppression first-hand gain that understanding?

I would suggest two methods. One is to study the Scriptural teaching on oppression. Get an NIV concordance, and read each of the 125-plus references to oppression. Another is to visit an impoverished community and witness the results of oppression. Have a member of that community take you on a tour and interpret what you see. Sit and listen to personal stories of oppression. Or better yet, move into such a community and live there for a year or two. While this is still a second-hand way to feel and understand the horror of oppression, it is better than nothing. The preferred approach, obviously, is to do both: study the Scriptures and spend time in an oppressed community.

Before we move on to the experiential portion of this chapter, let's spend a few more moments working out a Biblical definition of the term "oppression."

Earlier in the chapter, I introduced you to Thomas Hanks, the author of *God So Loved the Third World.* Now, a few quotations from Hanks on Biblical oppression:

Poverty is indicated in the context in 15 of the 20 occurrences of [*yanah*].

Nagas occurs 23 times in the Old Testament; 20 times with poverty...

---

[69] *The Wars of America*, ed. Ronald Wells (Grand Rapids, MI: Wm. B. Eerdmans Publishing Company, 1981).

Many of the uses of *nagas* in Exodus indicate how tampering with economic structures leads to oppression.

We should probably regard *daka* as the strongest Hebrew word denoting oppression. Both literally and etymologically *daka* means pulverize or crush... occurs 31 times... 10 times with the poor. **Oppression smashes the body and crushes the human spirit. That is, God's image is pulverized like a moth crushed under a boot heel.**[70] (emphasis added)

From Hanks' analysis we learn that the phrase "poor and oppressed" is correct Biblically. We can also derive the following definition: **oppression is the cruel and unjust exercise of power and authority, usually through social institutions, to crush, humiliate, animalize, impoverish, enslave and/or kill persons created in the image of God.**

We are about to listen to the voices of several Afro Americans who have experienced oppression. For the experiences of other ethnic groups, see Ronald Takaki's two books: *Strangers from a Different Shore: A History of Asian Americans* and *A Different Mirror: A History of Multicultural America*. Gender oppression is another area not directly covered in this book. One of the downsides of the civil rights movement is that some of its leaders were religious male chauvinists. See Mary King's book, *Freedom Song*, for documentation and for the birth of a new period of feminism. One woman has stated it something like this: "Of all the oppressed groups in the world, it is usually the women in these oppressed groups who are most oppressed." (In addition, if you are interested in exploring issues of gender injustice and the experiences of minority ethnic groups besides Afro Americans, please visit our online forum at http://www.urban-verses.com/O2JJ.)

First, an illustration from the days of slavery. A booklet entitled *The Willie Lynch Letter and The Making of a Slave* describes the "scientific process of man breaking and slave

---

[70] Hanks 8-12.

making." According to Lynch, breaking a slave is similar to breaking a wild horse:

> Above all you cannot get them to work in the natural state. Hence both the horse and the nigger must be broken; that is break them from one form of mental life to another – keep the body and take the mind. In other words, break the will to resist.[71]

Now, further details on the breaking process of the African female slave:

> **We reversed nature by burning and pulling one civilized nigger apart and bull whipping the other to the point of death – all in her presence.** By her being left alone, unprotected, with the male image destroyed, the ordeal caused her to move from her psychological dependent state to a *frozen independent state.*
>
> **In this frozen psychological state of independence she will raise her male and female offspring in reversed roles. For fear of the young male's life, she will psychologically train him to be mentally weak and dependent but physically strong... What have you got? You've got the nigger woman out front and the men behind and scared. This is the perfect situation for sound sleep and economics.**[72]

Willie Lynch claims that if this process is followed carefully, productive slavery can continue for 300 years.

Dolphus Weary, in *I Ain't Comin' Back*, describes the impact of oppression and poverty on him and his family:

> No matter what I do, no matter how hard I work, I'll always be second-class here. The system is rigged against

---

[71] Willie Lynch, *The Willie Lynch Letter and The Making of a Slave* (Bensenville, IL: Lushena Books, Inc., 1999) 14.
[72] Lynch 18-19.

me, and I will always make just enough to get by, but never enough to get ahead. That's the way it is here, and it's never going to change.[73]

How bad was it when Dolphus was growing up in rural Mississippi?

Sharecropping...meant farming on land belonging to a white man. He'd supply the seed and fertilizer and such and the blacks would supply the labor. Then when the harvest came in, half the crop went to the landowner and half to the blacks, only first their half had to repay any debts they had incurred while the crop was growing.

It was a system that kept them mired in debt and poverty... In the years when the crop was poor, a sharecropper might get into debt and have to mortgage his mule, wagon, and other gear to his boss... For a lot of black sharecroppers, life became an endless string of debts, and in the end they were left with nothing... The white man also dominated the sharecropper through stores.[74]

Charles Evers, in his book, *Have No Fear*, describes the difference between black and white education in the Mississippi Delta in the 1930s and '40s. Evers states:

Each morning, the white kids boarded a shiny new yellow-and-black school bus. Medgar [Evers] and I walked to school, three miles each way shivering our way down muddy, icy roads, often without coat or proper shoes... As the white school bus drove past, the driver would slow down so the white kids could lean out the windows, jeer and spit at the dirty niggers, and throw rocks. They tried to force us off the road into a ditch, to make us dirty our

---

[73] Dolphus Weary, *I Ain't Comin' Back,* (Wheaton, IL: Tyndale House, 1997) 29.
[74] Weary 30.

clothes. When we reached school, more than likely we were muddy and damp… Often we were hungry, too.

When they arrived at school, they entered "a dirty one-room shack" with many holes in the roof. The rain came in and "cold winds cut right through that shack." After going for firewood, Medgar and Charles "came back to see one hundred kids shivering in their hand-me-downs." One room, 100 kids, two teachers, all cold; conditions that made it hard to study, to say the least. Texbooks, used and out-of-date, portrayed blacks as "beasts of burden, savages with strong backs and weak minds."[75] Imagine the damage done to children who experienced this inhuman, sub-standard treatment year after year.

Charles Evers also describes the horror of a lynching, and the impact this left upon him and his brother, Medgar:

> In a beautiful pasture, the mob hung Willie Tingle from a tree, took shotguns and shot his body right in half. When he was dead, the lynch mob laughed, cut him down from the tree, and stripped his body. They left his bloody clothes under the tree to remind us Negroes what happened when we got too fresh… Every day for months, Medgar and I saw those rotting, blood-stained clothes each time we passed that pasture. For months, we dreamed about those bloody clothes. To this day [1997], I can still close my eyes and see that lynching in 1932.[76]

Bryant Myers, in his book, *Walking with the Poor*, describes what years of poverty and oppression may do to Third World poor:

> Christian concludes his explanation of poverty by pointing out that captivity to god-complexes, deception by princi-

---

[75] Charles Evers, *Have No Fear,* (New York: John Wiley & Sons, 1997) 24.

[76] Evers 37.

palities and powers, and inadequacies in worldview result in a tragic marring of the identity of the poor… the poor are systematically excluded as actors… a lifetime of suffering, deception, and exclusion is internalized by the poor in a way that results in the poor no longer knowing who they truly are or why they were created. This is the deepest and most profound expression of poverty… This is spiritual and psychological poverty of the deepest kind, the root of fatalism.[77]

Elliot Liebow, in what may still be the best study of the poor-poor and the impact that poverty and oppression have on black men in Washington, DC, states:

Living on the edge of both economic and psychological subsistence, the streetcorner man is obliged to expend all his resources on maintaining himself for the moment.[78]

A recurring theme of Liebow's book is the profound and continuing sense of failure, shame and low self-esteem that flows from oppression and poverty. Every human relationship – his wife, his children, etc. – reminds him of his failure as a person. He cannot live with these failures, so as much as he would like to have a normal life, job and marriage, he cuts and leaves.

John Perkins, in *A Quiet Revolution*, describes the impact of oppression in the form of racism and poverty on the people of Mississippi. Even worse than the poor shacks and lack of food was "the feeling of being trapped," or "the cycle of poverty" that flows out of generations of poverty and oppression. Miss Hester and her 10 children were caught in that trap:

Poverty had moved beyond her physical condition to claim her whole mind. For the real poor poverty means thinking

---

[77] Myers 76.

[78] Elliot Liebow, *Tally's Corner: A Study of Negro Streetcorner Men,* (Boston: Little, Brown & Co., 1967) 65.

just for the moment. It is the inability to think about the future because of the total demand to think about survival in the present. It is a culture, a whole way of life. A little money can't help much.[79]

John provides a vivid illustration of the fragile nature of life lived in poverty:

I remember that when we used to try to make houses out of playing cards, stacking and balancing just right, the least wrong movement or puff of wind or cough and they'd fall. And for the masses of black people in Mississippi, life is being lived in a house of cards. All of the things that give structure to life – education, employment, income, health, housing, leadership, transportation, nutrition – are for the most part flimsy excuses for survival, built upon and against each other, so that when one falls they all fall, and are rebuilt only to fall again.[80]

David Hesselgrave, retired professor of missions at Trinity Evangelical Seminary, wrote an article in the *Evangelical Missions Quarterly* entitled "The Poor: A Case of Mistaken Identity?" His interpretation of what the Scriptures teach about the poor flies in the face of what Hamer, Weary, Evers and Perkins have experienced.

Hesselgrave is concerned about the fact that the evangelical paradigm on poverty since 1970 has focused on being economically poor, "the poverty-stricken, disenfranchised, suffering and helpless people who constitute the underclass of society."[81] Hesselgrave asserts that the primary meaning of poor in both the Old and New Testaments is figurative or spiritual – "poor in

[79] John Perkins, *A Quiet Revolution* (Waco, TX: Word Books, 1976) 82.

[80] Perkins 87.

[81] David Hesselgrave, "The Poor: A Case of Mistaken Identity?" *Evangelical Missions Quarterly* Apr. 2003: 34.

spirit," "the pious poor," "the humble poor," "the godly poor." Only secondarily are the poor economically poor. He even interprets the reference to oppression in Luke 4:18 as "primarily figurative."[82] "To release the oppressed" is a phrase drawn from Isaiah 58:6. The context in the chapter is one of real poverty and real oppression. Isaiah has strong words about supposedly spiritual people who engage in oppression or who neglect the poor. Genuinely spiritual people break the cords of oppression.

Though the Hesselgrave article appears to be a scholarly analysis of the Scriptures, it is pathetically one-sided and an insult to the poor and oppressed of the world. In the Bible, the primary cause of poverty is oppression. The Bible exhorts us to "execute justice" on behalf of the poor and oppressed. It is inexcusable in this day and age to claim to do a Biblical study of the poor, yet basically ignore what the Bible teaches about oppression and justice in relation to the poor.

Victims of Oppression or Actors for Justice?

This final section of the chapter will take a somewhat different direction than the previous parts of the chapter.

Let's consider the question, "Who's responsible for working to end oppression?" In our nation, there are many groups that have suffered from abuse, mistreatment, exploitation and oppression. Many children have been neglected and abused; women are often harassed or exploited; Afro Americans have suffered from centuries of slavery and segregation; and the list goes on. Those of us with influence in our society should exert enormous efforts to stop oppression of all kinds, to create a just society.

Having said this, we must also acknowledge the victim's responsibility. In large part, the civil rights movement is the story of the oppressed rising up, even at great risk of job, life and limb, and nonviolently demanding change. The victims took the initiative; the oppressed acted.

---

[82] Hesselgrave 35.

Yes, the oppressors should repent and change. Unfortunately, they seldom do. The oppressed can languish in their oppression and cry, "Woe is me!" Or they can rise up and act.

Orlando Patterson, esteemed Harvard historical sociologist and author of *The Ordeal of Integration*, asserts that the present state of Afro Americans has been overly racialized, and made overly deterministic, by many scholars and by many Afro-American leaders.[83] His assessment is that today the cry of racism is too often and too widely used. We need a better balance between personal responsibility and social justice. Past and present oppression is tragically real, powerful and damaging. But it is not the last word. Patterson is very critical of both conservatives and liberals. See his fine book for a lengthy and fearless discussion.

---

[83] Orlando Patterson, *The Ordeal of Integration* (Washington, DC: Civitas Counterpoint, 1997) Chapters 2 & 3.

Pressed

Injustice ran deep
Infusing a tangled web of well-concealed roots
With invisible
Insidious
And insatiable
Poison

Still the blossoms sprang up
Stunted, but straining valiantly
Toward the beckoning sun

Some
Cut off and crushed
Yielded a pungent perfume
While others were pressed
Lovely
But lifeless
Between the pages of the family Bible

Chapter Five

Jubilee Justice

Let justice flood the land...
Amos 5:24 (Noble paraphrase)

It seems to be difficult for American evangelical Christians to understand and implement justice. Why is that? What are the barriers to justice?

1. Individualism is a rampant American value; justice is primarily a social concept. Individualism cuts the legs out from underneath justice. Individualism leads to an emphasis on personal salvation, but a neglect of social justice.

2. Because of individualism, we tend to think that charity is an adequate solution to a problem. Charity will always be needed, but unless it is accompanied by justice, which requires major social change, it is a weak and incomplete response to poverty and oppression. An example: There has been a massive church response to Hurricane Katrina – a natural catastrophe. This could be called the church's finest (charity) hour. But for many generations, we have had an ongoing social catastrophe in the Delta – the poorest region in the United States. There has been comparatively little church response to *this* disaster. A deep understanding of justice would have brought about a massive response to the poverty and oppres-

sion in the Delta – and, for that matter, in New Orleans prior to Katrina.

3. In the Old Testament, Hebrews had a strong sense of community; a good Hebrew would understand that love requires one to do justice, but most American Christians do not grasp that Biblical love demands justice. Righteousness and justice were like Siamese twins in the Old Testament. A Hebrew could not claim to be personally righteous and neglect social justice.

4. A shallow understanding of oppression results in a shallow understanding and practice of justice. Since oppression is missing in white evangelical theology and preaching, Biblical justice is not well understood.

5. The King James Version was the dominant English translation of the Bible for several centuries. In this version, the word "justice" appears seldom in the Old Testament and not at all in the New Testament. *Mishpat* is almost always translated as judgment, not justice. (For example, Amos 5:24 is rendered: "Let judgment roll down like waters…") Fortunately the New King James Version has corrected this huge mistake. The NKJV, the RSV and the NIV are all much superior to the Old King James on justice. Can you imagine how much damage was done by this justice omission? If you are someone who loves the KJV style, please switch to the NKJV.

6. The translators of classical Greek usually translated *dikaiosune* as justice, but strangely translators of New Testament Greek have generally translated *dikaiosune* as righteousness. So we do not see justice in our New Testaments very often.

7. Quirks in the English language. The Romance languages – Portuguese, Spanish, French, Latin, Italian and Greek – all have one word for justice/righteousness, and the primary meaning is justice. So a reader of the Bible in these languages will find the concept of justice much more often than a reader of English translations would find it.

8. I believe that almost all Americans, including most evangelical Christians, are contaminated by the American trinity of individualism, materialism and ethnocentrism. We range from being mildly sick to deathly ill. The American trinity is so deep and pervasive that it sometimes seems like Biblical justice doesn't stand a chance.

This is a formidable list of barriers, so it will not be easy for American evangelical Christians to understand fully and practice comprehensively Biblical justice. Nevertheless, I am convinced that we have a responsibility to make the attempt, and I also believe that God will help us to grasp this concept that is so very important to Him.

Jubilee Justice

Back to Biblical basics on justice. The best place that I know to begin is with the Sabbatical/Jubilee laws. The aim, the goal, of the Jubilee laws was that there should be no poor in the community/society. Is this a utopian goal, but not a very realistic one? Would it really be possible to eliminate poverty in a society? God not only said that it should be so, but He also showed Israel what to do to achieve this ideal.

First, stop lifelong, even generational, patterns of oppression. Frequently, every seven years, cancel debts and free slaves. The first requirement of justice is to stop oppression, to set people free from captivity. This is to be done systematically, according to law, not left to the whims of an individual person. That is the second step: the laws of the society are to be written to favor the poor, not to favor the rich. The poor are to be charged no interest.

Listen to some of the concerns people brought to Nehemiah (5:1-5): "We are mortgaging our fields, our vineyards and our homes to get grain during the famine." "We have had to borrow money to pay the king's tax." "We have had to subject our sons and daughters to slavery." Now, hear how Nehemiah addressed those responsible for the oppression (5:6-11):

> When I [Nehemiah] heard their outcry and these charges, I was very angry. You are exacting usury from your own countrymen... What you are doing is not right... Give back to them immediately their fields, vineyards, olive groves, and houses and also the usury you are charging them.

Nehemiah did not appoint a commission to study the matter and bring back a recommendation. Nehemiah called for the injustice to stop and (here's the third piece) for restitution to take place immediately. Our anger against injustice should prompt urgent action on our part. The church has the ability to organize and take quick action if it chooses to do so. The immediate and massive response to Hurricane Katrina proves this.

I've said before that Jubilee justice is two-pronged; it not only stops oppression and takes measures to prevent the recurrence of injustice, but it also provides access to resources from God's creation so a family can be self-sufficient. In an agricultural society, every family needs its own plot of land. Therefore, Jubilee justice requires that if, for some reason, a family loses its farm, every fifty years the land is to be returned to the family. Full justice is both negative and positive: it releases from oppression, and it provides resources for development.

Lincoln's freeing of the slaves was a very important action; it was the first step of justice. But it was not followed up by the second step – access to resources. Every freed slave family needed their own plot of land. Because Congress did not pass proposed "Forty Acres and a Mule" legislation, the freed slaves soon lost their freedom as they were subjected to the oppression of sharecropping and segregation. The failure to do complete justice had disastrous consequences.

Recently, the Virginia legislature passed unanimously an "apology" for slavery, but the apology does not "do justice." True repentance would have included restitution. So the descendants of slave owners get to keep the massive wealth earned through slavery.

Jubilee: Restoring Economic Justice

After this brief introduction of the Jubilee, its basic principles of justice and an indication of its importance, let us probe more deeply these remarkable God-given laws.

The Sabbatical year and the Jubilee year had the same basic purpose: to give every person/family access to the resources required to provide the necessities of life.

First, the Sabbatical year. The following Scriptural quotations are highlights from Deuteronomy 15, whose basic principle is that "at the end of every seven years you must cancel debts." (In the RSV, the phrase is, "grant a release"; the RSV uses the word release five times in the chapter.) The ideal was that there "should be no poor among you." There would not be if "you fully obey the Lord your God," because then "he will richly bless you."

However, because of the damage of sin, there will be some poor people. "If there is a poor man among your brothers freely lend him whatever he needs... Give generously... Supply him liberally... Give to him as the Lord your God has blessed you."

The message is: economic justice requires the periodic canceling of debts and generous giving to those in need. Could an economic system really work if the principle of **grace** is applied? Is **grace** a key to justice? In a capitalistic system, competition and profit militate against grace.

Second, more on the Jubilee. The following Scriptural quotations are highlights from Leviticus 25: "Count off seven sabbaths of years... Consecrate the fiftieth year and proclaim liberty throughout the land... It shall be a jubilee for you; each one of you is to return to his family property... The land must not be sold permanently, because the land is mine..."

Three times the people are warned not to take advantage of the powerless poor, and not to oppress them, or "rule over them ruthlessly..."

Now, a look at the insights of three experts on the Jubilee. First, Perry Yoder and his book, *Shalom*:

> The law tackled the matter of access to the economic resources in the Sabbatical and Jubilee laws. These laws were a type of economic reform legislation to redistribute the capital resources of the community so that they would not become concentrated in the hands of a few.[84]

Next, *The Upside-Down Kingdom*, by Donald Kraybill:

> As God's social blueprint for His people, the Jubilee dream put its finger on three major factors which generate socioeconomic inequality. Control of the land represents access to the natural resources. Ownership of slaves symbolizes the human labor necessary for production. Borrowing and lending money points to the management of capital and credit. The use of these three factors – natural resources, human resources, and financial capital – are keys to determining the amount of inequity in any society...
>
> Another part of the Jubilean genius is that it doesn't squelch individual initiative. It doesn't prescribe that all things should be held in common or that every one must have exactly the same amount... There are not two separate compartments for religion and economics.

---

[84] Yoder 81.

The two are woven together into one cloth in the Jubilee model.[85]

Our third expert on the Jubilee is Christopher Wright, author of *An Eye for An Eye*:

> The paradigmatic relevance of the jubilee and related land laws in the Old Testament is particularly applicable to situations where land tenure and land reform are pressing issues of social and political dispute. The jubilee was designed to prevent the accumulation of the bulk of the land in the hands of a few. It protected a system of land tenure that was intended to be broadly equitable, with the ownership of land widely spread throughout the population. It was an attempt to impede, and indeed periodically to reverse, the relentless economic forces that lead to a downward spiral of debt, poverty, dispossession and bondage.[86]

The essential message of the prophets was, "Do justice or face judgment." The people of Israel had forsaken the principles of Jubilee justice and were engaging in widespread oppression. Despite the warnings of prophet after prophet, the people refused to repent, so God sent them into exile.

In the King James Bible, we find the quaint but tragic phrase: "the noise of solemn assemblies." When is worship only a solemn assembly? When is beautiful praise music only noise? When are Bible study and prayer only empty words? When they are mixed with idolatry and oppression. When they are silent on justice. Who says so? The prophet, Amos, does. Amos says that God "cannot stand your assemblies... Away with the noise of your songs" (5:21-23). Only worship accompanied by justice is acceptable. Only majestic hymns accompanied by justice are acceptable. Only Bible study and prayer accompanied by justice are acceptable.

---

[85] Kraybill 101.

[86] Christopher Wright, *An Eye for an Eye* (Downers Grove, IL: InterVarsity Press, 1984) 130.

My favorite Afro-American woman lay theologian, Lee Harper, once declared regarding the Mississippi Delta: "Injustice ran deep and cloaked itself well among those things that appeared just." Off the coast of Ghana, a Reformed church was built on top of a slave dungeon. If that church was used for 100 years, 5200 sermons were preached. Did God ever hear, accept one word from those 5200 sermons, or was that church simply filled with the noise of solemn assemblies, while its basement was filled with the groaning of captives?

I spend much of my time in the Bible Belt, where the cross and resurrection are preached. People claim to be born again. People claim to believe the Bible from cover to cover. A church stands on nearly every corner. During the segregation era, injustice ran deep here and cloaked itself well with an apparently Biblically based religion. Was God ever pleased by the 'worship' in these churches?

When injustice ran deep, Wilberforce organized a team of the best people he could find and, after a lifetime, they stopped the slave trade and slavery in the British Empire.

When injustice ran deep, Martin Luther King organized a team of the best people he could find, and they broke the back of segregation in the American South.

Today, injustice runs deep in the form of the wealth gap – an oppressive, unjust 10-1 ratio. Who among us is going to organize a team to do justice? To work at closing that wealth gap until we attain equality?

In the midst of massive injustice, Amos issued a clarion call (5:24):

> Let justice roll on like a river,
> righteousness like a never failing stream

Habakkuk also issued a call (my paraphrase):

> In the midst of massive injustice, continue to live righteously and do justice by faith – faith that the Sovereign God of the universe will do justice in due time.

From Isaiah 58, we hear this exhortation:

> to loose the chains of injustice...
> to set the oppressed free...
> to share your food with the hungry.

Is God pleased with modern American worship? Or is injustice running deep, and the church remaining silent? Is the church tolerating or even participating in the wealth gap? Away with the noise of our solemn assemblies. It is time to act, to do justice. Who will lead the way?

Social Justice in the New Testament

A former colleague of mine who taught Bible used to say that the Old Testament was full of justice, but that the social justice message disappeared in the New Testament and was replaced by personal salvation. On the surface, a good argument could be made for this position. So what evidence is there that social justice is a New Testament theme as well?

First, a look at the Greek word *dikaiosune*. This word has commonly been translated as righteousness in English, but some good scholars are asserting that it could be translated as justice.

* When Hebrew is translated into Greek (the Septuagint), the translators usually use the Greek word *dikaiosune* to communicate the Hebrew for justice.

* As the classical Greek *dikaiosune* is translated into English, it is commonly translated as justice.

* The Romance languages – Portuguese, Spanish, French, Italian, Latin – all have one word for justice/righteousness, and the primary meaning is that of justice.

* Some scholars, such as Glen Stassen, David Gushee and Joseph Grassi, argue that *dikaiosune* should be translated as justice in the Sermon on the Mount. If this were to be done, the Beatitude would read, "Blessed are those

who hunger and thirst after justice..." or the Stassen/Gushee paraphrase, "Blessed are those who hunger and thirst for a justice that delivers and restores to covenant community, for God is a God who brings such justice."[87] And Matthew 6:33 would read: "Seek first the kingdom and its justice..."

* The New English Bible does translate *dikaiosune* as justice in Matthew 6:33. And Romans 14:17 is rendered: "The kingdom of God is justice..."

Joseph Grassi, author of *Informing the Future: Social Justice in the New Testament*, asserts that there is a strong social justice message in the New Testament that is rooted and grounded in the Old Testament: "Social Justice in the New Testament grows out of models presented in the Old Testament."[88]

One of Grassi's more innovative chapters is entitled "Matthew: The Gospel of Justice." No other Bible scholar that I know of has ever strongly tied Matthew to justice. At the time that Matthew wrote, there were a few rich households and many poor people. Justice was a burning issue. In this context, Grassi argues that the Greek word *dikaiosune*, usually translated as righteousness in most English translations, ought to be translated as justice. If so, then the Sermon on the Mount is suddenly pervaded with justice; two major and related themes surface – the **kingdom of God and justice.**

Grassi notes the close tie between Isaiah and Matthew; Matthew quotes Isaiah six times, and Isaiah is the prophet of justice. According to Grassi, "justice has two arms: equal sharing of possessions and right relationships."[89]

One of the first issues addressed in the Spirit-filled church in Acts was a justice issue – a rich-poor gap. Palestine was full of poor people. Many of the new converts were poor. So the

---

[87] Stassen and Gushee 43.

[88] Grassi 101.

[89] Grassi 152.

rich people in the church responded to the need in such a generous fashion, by selling houses and lands, that the Scripture records that there were no poor among them. A remarkable act of generosity and justice – an important mark of a Spirit-filled person. (Next time you look at the familiar passage at the end of Acts 4, begin your reading in verse 31 rather than verse 32.) The opposite of justice is oppression. Who are the greedy oppressors? Literally, they are idiots who hoard wealth. The Greek phrase "*ta idia*" means "one's own." Having enough to be self-sufficient in terms of the necessities of life is fine, but piling up more and more of "one's own" is idiocy. It may be a part of the American dream, but it is idiocy. Gathering in and hoarding wealth is stupid and dangerous; it is idolatrous and addictive. Therefore, one is an idiot to do so.

Charles Avila, a Catholic priest born and trained in the Philippines, grew up believing the dominant view that the poor were poor because they were ignorant, lazy, superstitious, and resistant to change. Not many in the Church questioned this – the rich were rich, and the poor were poor, this was life. Some charity may be needed, but no fundamental change was possible.

But then Avila got to know some of the landless peasants firsthand. A whole new perspective on the causes of poverty began to emerge. Social injustice tied to the lack of ownership of land seemed to be the key. The landless tenants worked hard, very hard, but always ended up in debt to the landlord. He owned the land; he dictated the financial arrangements. Avila comments:

> The mighty were the big landlords who also became the big capitalists: middlemen, money lenders, bureaucrats, and industrialists. Ownership of land led to ownership of various kinds of capital. Because of the agrarian nature of the economy, land wealth was the prime source of all wealth and privilege, and the basic status of the deprived and oppressed was landless.[90]

---

[90] Charles Avila, *Ownership: Early Christian Teaching* (Maryknoll, NY: Orbis Books, 1983) xvi.

Avila began to wonder what ownership meant, and what the early Church fathers said about ownership. So he wrote a dissertation on the topic, which was later published as *Ownership: Early Christian Teaching*. He discovered "two fundamentally different approaches to the understanding of ownership." One was a social/legal approach; the other was a moral/philosophical approach. The Church father John Chrysostom was deeply concerned about the problems of ownership. He asked: "But what is the meaning of 'mine' and 'not mine'?... chilly words which introduce innumerable wars into the world." [91]

Augustine and others were worried about Roman law and its protection of private property, which they felt had been abused. This raises a question: Is small-scale land ownership, each individual farmer owning his or her own land, justified, while large-scale land ownership by landlords, agri-businesses or multinational corporations is not? Avila summarizes Augustine's thoughts:

> Augustine lived in fourth-century Roman Africa, where Roman law theory and practice of private property had led, quite naturally, to the possession by a few persons of very great wealth, at the price of the dispossession and impoverishment of very many other persons. This theological giant of the patristic age saw the prevailing oppression, the blatant injustices perpetrated against the poor, as an assault on Christ!... He argued that this legalized right was an affront...to the absolute dominion and paternal providence of the Creator, who had willed all of creation to be all in common, according to each person's need...[92]

Clement of Alexandria called for a balance between *autarkeia* (self-sufficiency) and *koinonia* (sharing, fellowship in

---

[91] Avila 122.
[92] Avila 37.

community). After a basic self-sufficiency is obtained, the primary emphasis must be on *koinonia*. Clement states:

> It is God himself who has brought our race [humankind] to a *koinonia*, by sharing Himself, first of all, and by sending His word (Logos) to all alike, and by making all things for all. Therefore, everything is common and the rich should not grasp a greater share. The expression, then, "I own something and I have more than enough; why should I not enjoy it?" is not worthy of a human nor does it indicate any community feelings. The other expression does, however: "I have something; why should I not share it with those in need?" Such a one is perfect, and fulfills the command: "Thou shalt love thy neighbor as thyself."[93]

Basil the Great says that land, rain and sun are *koina*, a part of nature to be available to all. *Koina* are to be used to promote *koinonia*. *Ta koina* (common goods) are contrasted with *ta idia* (one's own things). Basil warns that one should not make private, one's own, what should be public, for the common use of all. Further, Basil warns:

> The private appropriation of the *koina*, such as land, is robbery. Hence, continued excessive landownership is but fresh and continued theft. Indeed, the hoarding of other things, too, which one does not need, but what others do need, is itself a form of theft.[94]

It sounds like the Church fathers had something in common with the church described in the book of Acts (4:32-35):

> All the believers were one in heart and mind. No one claimed that any of his possessions was his own, but they shared everything they had... There were no needy persons among them. For from time to time those who owned

---

[93] Ibid.
[94] Avila 55.

land or houses sold them, brought the money from the sales and put it at the apostles' feet, and it was distributed to anyone as he had need.

For those readers who would like to dig deeper into Biblical justice, I would highly recommend *Shalom*, by Perry Yoder; Yoder, an Old Testament scholar, creates a socioeconomic ethic based on the Biblical concepts of justice and shalom. Also, a previously mentioned book, *Kingdom Ethics*, by Glen Stassen and David Gushee; chapter 17, entitled "Justice," examines justice and injustice in the gospels, something not commonly done. Two superb books.

Finland: A Model of a Just Society?

Is it possible in our modern world to create a just society, one that is both productive and fair? Could a nation avoid the extremes of communism and unrestrained capitalism (the old Soviet Union and the modern U.S.)? Is there a better way, a middle ground? Possibly so. Consider the nation of Finland. Finland is a modern, competitive industrial economy that provides a wide range of social services to all of its residents. Most U.S. citizens would say that this can't be done, but maybe we should try to think outside the U.S. box. Humility is not a strong U.S. virtue; we tend to think we are the biggest and the best. Not always true.

> Finns have one of the world's most generous systems of state-funded educational, medical and welfare services… They pay nothing for education at any level, including medical school or law school. Their medical care, which contributes to an infant-mortality rate that is half of what ours is and a life-expectancy greater than ours, costs relatively little. (Finns devote 7 percent of gross domestic product to health care; we spend 15 percent.) Finnish senior citizens are well cared for.[95]

---

[95] Robert G. Kaiser, "In Finland's Footsteps: If we're so rich and smart, why aren't we more like them?" *The Washington Post* 7 Aug. 2005: B-1.

There is little poverty in Finland; we have 35,000,000 poor – 16,000,000 in extreme poverty. They have universal health care; we have 47,000,000 without health insurance. O.K., O.K., I know what you are going to say: they pay higher taxes than we do. That is true, but they end up with more equality and justice. That sounds more Biblical to me. (For the record, we pay around 30 percent in taxes; Finns pay about 50 percent in taxes.) And I am sure the Finns have nothing like our 10-1 wealth gap. The Finns had to reinvent themselves in order to achieve the above. I think that we are as smart as the Finns; we could reinvent ourselves, too.

The Flood

Would forty days and forty nights
Of ceaseless water
Be enough
To rid this land of all its sin?

In forty days and forty nights
Of desperate struggle
To survive
Would oppressor and oppressed find common ground?

After forty days and forty nights
Of relentless cleansing
And crying out
Would justice find a place to light?

Chapter Six

Deception Versus Truth

He is a liar and the father of lies
John 8:45

The truth will set you free
John 8:32

J ohn describes the Holy Spirit as the **Spirit of truth;** Jesus
described Satan as the "father of lies." Usually, oppression is
covered by deceit, by a web of lies, by clever ideological propaganda that uses good words such as shalom, freedom and
democracy to cover social evils.

In Jeremiah 5:27-28, the wicked oppressors are described
thus:

> Their houses are full of deceit;
> they have become rich and powerful,
> they do not defend the rights of the poor.

Or Jeremiah 6:13-14:

> From the least to the greatest,
> all are greedy for gain;
> prophets and priests alike,
> all practice deceit.
> They dress the wound of my people
> as though it were not serious.
> "Shalom, shalom," they say,
> when there is no shalom.

Jeremiah 7:1-8 describes the people coming to worship at the same time that they were engaging in oppression, trusting in mouthing deceptive words, "This is the temple of the Lord, this is the temple of the Lord, this is the temple of the Lord."

Much the same was happening in Jesus' time. Israel was highly religious, yet full of oppression. The oppression was covered over by religiosity. We desperately need the Spirit of truth to enable us to see the truth about oppression and justice. Remember, most of the people followed the comforting but deceptive words of the false prophets; the stern words of the true prophets – the call to do justice or face judgment – were dismissed.

After warning about cunning and crafty false teachers, full of deceitful schemes, Paul exhorts Christians to "speak the truth in love" (Eph. 4:15). Discerning the truth, distinguishing between the true and the false, is more complex and difficult than it appears on the surface. I am now 81 years old, and I have spent most of my adult life either studying at the college or graduate level or teaching at the college level. Most of my studying and teaching has been in evangelical Christian liberal arts colleges. I have sat under or been colleagues with some very bright people. I was taught many important truths.

Yet as I reflect back over the years, I am amazed at how often what I was taught was not the whole truth, the complete truth. Even in Christian circles, the truth was often limited, partial or one-sided. For example, for most of my life I have been on a pilgrimage to understand the nature of the kingdom of God. I have read what the evangelical experts had to say, but I always felt that something was missing, though I did not know at the time what that missing piece was. I read each new article or book on the kingdom with anticipation, only to be disappointed again and again. Only in the last few years do I feel reasonably content that I have finally grasped the present and social dimensions of the kingdom of God here on earth. But I am still looking for someone to tie the Holy Spirit, the kingdom of God and justice together in one package, reflecting my paraphrase of Romans 14:17, "The kingdom of God is…justice, shalom and joy in the Holy Spirit."

I write this not to discourage you from pursuing the truth, but to warn you that the search for truth is more difficult, demanding and time-consuming than you might realize. It may take years to understand and own some truths. An intelligent, Afro-American friend of mine, now deceased – a deeply committed Christian and pastor – had learned to be suspicious of the objectivity of many evangelical writers. On many subjects, he preferred to read a secular scholar, if possible, because of the one-sidedness of many evangelical authors.

I have developed an eight-hour seminar on a Biblically based theology of society, covering such issues as ethnocentrism, oppression, justice, shalom and the kingdom of God. I was invited to give this seminar to *Good Works, Inc.*, in Athens, Ohio, where they serve the homeless. Keith Wasserman, a converted Jew, is the executive director; he is far ahead of most people that I have met on the poor, justice, etc. But after the workshop, he wrote to me to tell me that in his 22 years of following Jesus, he had never encountered this perspective on the poor and oppressed.

I mention this not to puff my own seminar, but to indicate that the search for truth about the poor and oppressed can take many years: nearly a lifetime for me, and more than two decades for Keith Wasserman.

John is known as the apostle of love; he is also the apostle of truth. John exhorts us to "love…in truth" (3:8). The words true or truth occur at least 10 times in his first epistle. Synonyms of truth such as testimony, message or commandments are found another 15-20 times. And many sharp contrasts are drawn between what is a lie and what is the truth. Only after John has again and again discussed truth in terms of light and darkness, Jesus versus the anti-Christ, and sin versus righteousness, does he move on to detailed exhortations to love. Love without truth has no backbone, no direction. To act wisely in love, a person must be grounded in truth.

So remember, be alert. Distortions and deceptions abound. Probably the most dangerous mistruths are half-truths. Good Biblical words can be twisted to deceive the hearer (for an example, look at Luke 4:10-11 to see how the devil even attempted to draw Jesus astray through a misapplication of Scripture).

Pentecostals have rediscovered the neglected truth of the person, power and gifts of the Holy Spirit – an enormously important contribution to the church. Yet, according to Derek Prince, a charismatic leader, if the Spirit's blessing is not transferred out into the larger society (in other words, if the Spirit's power is not related to justice and the kingdom of God), then Pentecostalism degenerates into "spiritual self-indulgence." Prince describes a two-hour service in which the supernatural presence and blessing of the Holy Spirit was powerfully evident:

> We had touched God; His power was at our disposal. God spoke to my spirit and said, "Do not let them make the same mistake that Pentecostals have so often made in the past by squandering My power in **spiritual self-indulgence**. Tell them to pray for the future of Kenya."[96] (emphasis added)

The congregation *did* intercede for the troubled nation of Kenya. Prince is convinced that this is one of the reasons that Kenya, once torn by colonialism and racial strife, became one of the most stable nations in Africa (for a time).

Spiritual self-indulgence. A strange and tragic phrase. How could anyone misuse the precious Holy Spirit? Yet we know from the Bible that the Corinthian church did a similar thing; they pursued the gifts of the Spirit for self-edification, rather than for the edification of the church.

Spiritual self-indulgence. Did this prepare the way for material self-indulgence – the prosperity gospel which is now

---

[96] Derek Prince, *Shaping History Through Prayer and Fasting* (Revell, 1973) 70.

widespread in some Pentecostal circles? Would a close relationship between the Holy Spirit and the kingdom of God as social justice have prevented this? Would this have channeled the power of the Spirit outward to the poor and oppressed?

National/ethnic self-indulgence. The Afrikaners saw themselves as a chosen people, called to set up a Christian nation. While Afrikaners ruled, they kept the Sabbath day holy (in a strict legalistic sense), abortion was low, pornography was low, and church attendance was high. Sounds like a Christian paradise! But we all know the rest of the story. Their sense of chosenness led to an arrogant ethnocentrism. This, in turn, led to systematic oppression of black South Africans. They preached the cross and the resurrection. What was missing from their brand of the gospel that allowed them to distort the Christian faith so badly?

Ethnic self-indulgence. White Southerners created the Bible Belt, primarily a Baptist Bible Belt. They claimed to believe the Bible from cover to cover; they preached the cross and the resurrection; they claimed to be born again. Some were Spirit-filled. There was a church on almost every corner, so to speak. A generation or two ago, "almost everybody" in the white community went to church; "almost everybody" in the black community went to church. But, again, we know the rest of the story. Racism, oppression and poverty were rampant. What was missing from the Bible Belt gospel? Or what had been added to the gospel that didn't belong there?

Ethnic self-indulgence. In the early 1900s, the Pentecostal movement began at Azusa Street. Many ethnic groups from all over the Los Angeles area gathered in a barn, and all were filled with the Holy Spirit. Ethnic divisions were broken down, miracle of all miracles. The human instrument of this revival was an Afro American by the name of Seymor.

A Euro-American friend of his came to see what God was doing, but he was appalled by the "racial mixing." His Klan-like theories opposing racial mixing led him to oppose Seymor. So he withdrew and started his own pure white Pentecostal movement. He started preaching a mixed gospel of racial purity and Spirit-filling. Why God did not strike him dead on the spot as he did Ananias and Sapphira, I do not know, but He did not, and the Pentecostal Church became as segregated as the rest of the American Church.

The Power of Culture

Culture has an incredible power to shape our thinking and values. Romans 12:2 says, "Don't let the world squeeze you into its own mold." Or, "Don't let the world brainwash you into accepting its values."

Culture possession can be as evil, as demonic, as personal demon possession. Only a small percentage of persons in a society actually become demon possessed, but nearly everyone in a culture is poisoned by negative cultural values. If a person is born into a racist culture and lives in that culture for her/his first eighteen years, such a person is "predestined" to become a racist, to some degree. And that person might also believe that this racist social system is ordained by God.

It is my conviction that modern American culture is pervaded by the negative values of the American Trinity – individualism, materialism, and ethnocentrism – and that most American evangelical Christians attempt to serve two trinities, the Christian trinity and the American trinity, at the same time. I also believe that most American evangelical Christians are not aware of what they are doing, nor do they realize the deep conflict between the two trinities.

Another way of expressing the power that culture has over our lives is to say that with every breath of cultural air we take in, we are gradually poisoned with negative cultural values. The process is slow, quiet and subtle, so that we are usually unaware of what is going on. But over time the amount of cultural poison we absorb is large – large enough to make us sick. However, this sickness may appear to be quite normal, because everyone around us is also sick.

There is a culture war going on in America, but the real war is not between the religious right and the secular left; it is between the American culture and the kingdom of God. Unless kingdom of God concepts and values are pervading our lives, and frankly I don't see much evidence of this, we are almost automatic victims of our culture.

Allow me to illustrate this assertion using the life of General Lee Butler, former commander of our nation's nuclear forces. The following is from an interview with General Butler published in *Sojourners* magazine. Butler was born and raised in Mississippi:

> As a child, it was a burden that I never understood, and did not perceive or feel until my later formative years, after I had gone off to the Academy. Only then did it dawn on me that the society in which I had grown up was so tortured and morally debased by its deep racial divisions.

> I have spent years going back over that historical terrain trying to imagine how it was that I was so indifferent to a world where blacks and whites went to different schools, drank from different water fountains, rode in different seats on public transportation. Where blacks were considered chattel property, were abused and even murdered on whims. All of that was accepted as not just normal but the rightful scheme of things. It was not until I was a young adult and had left that environment permanently that it finally came crashing home how despicable were these circumstances.

Then General Butler entered another culture with equal power to brainwash a person, and he fell into the same trap again; this time, the military culture got him.

> The parallels with respect to my attitudes toward nuclear weapons are very strong, as today I strive to understand how we came to normalize the process of shearing away an entire society, to accept as a routine price of deterrence

slaughtering populations wholesale. We not only treated these policies and practices as normal, but invented sophisticated theoretical schemes and strategic underpinnings to structure this normalcy. In many respects, we elevated it to a theology. I think that there are very powerful analogies between dealing with the legacy of racism and the belief systems of nuclear deterrence. [97]

So we see from the life of General Butler, Christian though he was (or was he?), that he was the victim of two brainwashings. First, the brainwashing by his Mississippi culture; then, the nuclear arms brainwashing by his military culture. Fortunately, he was eventually freed from both of these non-Christian ideologies or idolatries, **but not before he served them for many years as an oppressor or potential oppressor.** Unfortunately, many American "Christians" go to their deaths still believing in the idolatrous values of racism and militarism.

---

[97] David Cortright, "An Unexpected Calling: An interview with Gen. George Lee Butler," *Sojourners* Jan/Feb 1999.

Truth

The lie shifts like sand beneath my feet
And whispers in one treacherous, insubstantial breath
That I am at once both worthless and superior –
So flawed that my contribution to God's work
    is more hindrance than help
And yet so much better than the next –
    for a myriad of reasons –
    that I need not consider as neighbor
    anyone who fails to reflect an image of myself

I dig frantically through the shards of stone
    and strike at last a solid rock
At first it seems an obstacle
    a source of pain to bloodied fingertips
    and too heavy a burden for such frail shoulders
    as mine
But as I regard it skeptically
    its surface shimmers into focus
    and two perfectly-formed hollows invite
    my weary soles
    to find a place to rest

Chapter Seven

The Spirit and the Kingdom of God

The **agenda** of the kingdom of God is **justice**;
the **dynamic** of the kingdom of God is the **Holy Spirit**.

Graham Cray

The **kingdom of God is justice, shalom, and joy in the Holy Spirit.**

Rom. 14:17 (Noble paraphrase)

First, a review of some concepts we've already encountered, before we plunge into the relationship between the Holy Spirit and the kingdom of God. Mortimer Zuckerman wrote the following in an October 2, 2006, editorial in the conservative *U.S. News and World Report*:

> The income gap between the richest and poorest Americans is wider than at any time in history, and we must take urgent measures to begin closing it.[98]

In a December 25, 2006 / January 1, 2007 editorial, Zuckerman, a "secular prophet," asserts:

> Millions of Americans worry that they're just one health crisis away from financial ruin. We must find a way to provide all with effective health insurance.[99]

---

[98] Zuckerman, "For a Fairer America."

[99] Mortimer Zuckerman, "America's High Anxiety," *U.S. News and World Report* 25 Dec. 2006/1 Jan. 2007: 100.

Kevin Phillips, another conservative "secular prophet," worries that "concentrated ownership" may ruin American democracy. Phillips is deeply concerned about the wealth gap.

These secular prophets raise the issue of justice, or the lack thereof, in American society.

"Justice is broken" declares the Christian Reformed Church's document on restorative justice.[100] How do we stop oppression and create the conditions for shalom in a community/society? By doing justice, executing justice, establishing justice, restoring justice, according to the Scriptures. Justice is setting things right, righting wrongs.

Justice is a holistic concept; it has social, economic, political and religious components. The Old Testament ties justice and righteousness together; they cannot be separated. Righteousness is the standard, the norm. Justice is an action word. Justice restores what is broken. Justice restores to a state of righteousness.

God loves justice. God hates oppression. When we talk about justice, we cannot, we must not, sugarcoat the issues. As Karen Lebacqz asserts, we seek justice in the context of an unjust world.[101] Lebacqz studied justice in her Harvard doctoral dissertation. She essentially concluded that the great scholars of justice were deficient in their understanding of justice because they did not begin with injustice, oppression.

As Christians, we should not sanitize our history; rather, Christians should lead our nation in confessing our many social evils, our sins of oppression – poverty, sexism, racism, militarism, slavery, etc. Then and only then will the lovely phrase "with liberty and justice for all" have meaning for all. Then and

---

[100] *Committee to Study Restorative Justice*, Christian Reformed Church, 2005. Go to http://www.crcna.org/pages/osjha_restorative.cfm to download the committee's report.

[101] Karen Lebacqz, *Justice in an Unjust World* (Minneapolis: Augsburg Publishing House, 1987).

only then will Lincoln's eloquent description of "a government of the people, by the people, and for the people" have meaning for all. These words will not be hollow if we **"let justice roll down like waters and righteousness like an everflowing stream." May Jubilee justice flood over America and wash the garbage of oppression away.**

Do you remember Luke 4:18-19 and the four key concepts: **the Spirit, the poor, the oppressed and Jubilee justice?** When these four Biblical concepts are central in a church's ministry, then a measure of the kingdom of God has been incarnated here on earth. This chapter will focus on the relationship between the Holy Spirit and the kingdom of God. The Spirit and the kingdom have largely been divorced in the evangelical church, possibly because most evangelicals have overly futurized and spiritualized the kingdom of God. We see the kingdom only as something that will come at the end of time. We have neglected the present and social dimensions of the kingdom. If the kingdom is future, then we do not need the Holy Spirit. If the kingdom is present and social, a justice issue, then we desperately need the person, power and wisdom of the Holy Spirit.

If we are serious about imitating and following Jesus, we need the anointing of the Holy Spirit to preach good news to the poor. We also need the anointing of the Holy Spirit to release the oppressed. And we need the anointing of the Spirit to incarnate Jubilee justice in a community/society.

Let us begin with the first of the four key concepts: **the Spirit.** There are various ministries of the Holy Spirit: power, the fruit of the Spirit, the gifts of the Spirit, and the Spirit as teacher of truth. All are important, but in this chapter, I am going to zero in on the Spirit of truth. Why? Because we can't intelligently bring the power of the Spirit to bear on oppression/justice issues if we can't distinguish between ideological propaganda and truth about the poor. Many Christians do not understand why the poor are poor. The church cannot bring the gifts of the Spirit to bear on oppression/justice issues if they do not know the Biblical truth about oppression. If we continue in our Biblical, historical and sociological ignorance, we may end up doing more harm than good.

Oppression can be defined as the cruel and unjust exercise of power and authority. The Holy Spirit is God's power and authority to break the bondages of oppression, to incarnate justice in society. This is a huge challenge, so great that often as humans we feel a sense of hopelessness as we face the mountains of oppression. How do we even begin to chip away at a 10-1 wealth gap? Only the Holy Spirit can empower us to break down these oppressions. Casting out social evils such as ethnocentrism and oppression will be far more difficult than casting out a single evil spirit from one individual.

The Kingdom of God

We have already looked in some depth at our fearsome opposition – the father of lies, deception and culture; now we move on to the Biblical alternative – the **kingdom of God.**

We are concerned about the here and now, present society, so we will be emphasizing the present and social dimensions of the kingdom of God. We need a clear and compelling understanding of the kingdom of God if we are to have any chance of overcoming our opposition.

Over a period of several years, I have asked a wide variety of people to write down a one-sentence definition of the kingdom of God. Those asked included Pentecostal and Reformed, young and old, Afro-American and Euro-American, and everyone else in between. I have asked the cream of the crop – those who attend a workshop at a CCDA conference. I have asked Afro-American pastors.

I discovered that there is no clear consensus – no clear and compelling vision – of the kingdom of God. Most definitions were vague and imprecise. They tended to be future and spiritual in their orientation. The kingdom of God does have a future component: it will fully come with the Second Coming of Jesus

Christ. Obviously, the kingdom has a spiritual component: one enters the kingdom by being born again. What was missing from most of the definitions was a sharp present and social dimension. For example, only one in ten, generously interpreted, included anything on justice. Few of the definitions had enough clarity, sharpness or specificity to challenge a person to want to commit his/her life to incarnate the kingdom of God here on earth. John Perkins commented once that it seemed like this was the first time a group had given serious thought to the kingdom of God.

But when I give the same people a copy of the Messianic passages from Isaiah and ask them to redo their definitions, they shine. The difference between their two definitions is like night and day. Justice takes center stage, the poor are included, and even the Spirit is often mentioned. One time I had a Princeton Seminary graduate in a workshop; he said the Messianic passages were the single most helpful thing at the workshop. See chapter two for a list of the Messianic passages.

In a review of 20th century scholarly theological literature on the kingdom of God, Marcus Borg concludes that for most of the century the future/spiritual or eschatological emphasis dominated the discussion. Even in the C.H. Dodd emphasis on the kingdom as present, "the futurist element…remained dominant. *Because* the future coming was so near, the Kingdom was also present."[102] Borg's conclusion: the theologians had not provided a "clear and compelling" vision of the kingdom of God for the church. My conclusion: because the church lacked a clear and compelling vision of the kingdom of God, this left a theological vacuum which the American trinity of individualism, materialism and ethnocentrism rushed in to fill.

When Borg discussed the dominant future/spiritual paradigm of the kingdom of God, there was no mention of the Holy Spirit. But by 1986, the "imminent futurist consensus had faded

---

[102] Marcus Borg, "Jesus and the Kingdom of God," *The Christian Century* 22 Apr. 1987: 380.

away," at least among the more liberal scholars. A new synthesis was developing – "an understanding of the Kingdom that is simple, comprehensive and pregnant with meaning for the life of the church."[103] Though Borg does not say this, the practice of the kingdom of God in the Civil Rights Movement may have stimulated this new theological emphasis.

I would like to label this new paradigm "present and social," though it continues to have a spiritual component; this name would distinguish it from the past overly spiritual and overly future emphasis. Borg states that the present/social paradigm is highlighted by an image of God as King, as in God's kingship over Israel:

> The image of God as King had a twofold meaning: it pointed to the divine majesty, to God's power and lordship; and it pointed to a **way of life** lived in response to that power and lordship.[104] (emphasis added)

Only when Borg begins to discuss the kingdom of God as present and social does the Holy Spirit come to the forefront of the discussion. The Holy Spirit becomes the key to the incarnation of the kingdom of God here on earth. Borg asserts that the kingdom of God not only refers to the reign of God, a common short definition of the kingdom of God, "but also to the life lived in response to God as King."

According to Borg, the principles of life tied into incarnating the kingdom of God are sharply contrasted with the "conventional wisdom" of culture. Every culture (the *cosmos* or social order in the New Testament) presents us with a picture of reality. But Jesus, in his teachings about the kingdom of God, became a subversive radical; he called into question "their understanding and loyalties, and [invited] them to participate in another way – namely life under the kingship of God."

---

[103] Borg 381.
[104] Borg 382.

Borg's judgment is that the American church has largely failed to understand the nature of the kingdom of God and failed to tie the person, power and wisdom of the Holy Spirit to incarnating the kingdom of God here on earth. The result:

> The church to a large extent participates in our culture's conventional wisdom, indeed often legitimating it. Much of contemporary American Christianity is "enculturated religion," radically adapted to culture and domesticated within it. We live in a Babylon often declared to be Zion.[105]

I encourage you to read Marcus Borg's brilliant three-page article in its entirety.

In a small but powerful book, Howard Snyder examines the present and social dimensions of the kingdom of God by tracing key Old Testament themes such as shalom, justice and the Jubilee. Snyder warns:

> Through our traditions we have voided the Word of God (Mk. 7:13) and its kingdom message. Many people who have been converted to Jesus seemingly have never been converted to the kingdom he proclaimed.[106]

Snyder ties the Holy Spirit and the kingdom of God together in this provocative paraphrase of Acts 1:6-8:

> Now, after the resurrection, his disciples ask, "Are you *finally* going to set up your kingdom?" ...[Jesus responds:] "The time for the full flowering of the new order still remains a mystery to you; it's in God's hands. But...the Holy Spirit will give you the power to live the kingdom

---

[105] Ibid.

[106] Howard Snyder, *A Kingdom Manifesto: Calling the Church to Live under God's Reign* (Downers Grove, IL: InterVarsity Press, 1985) Preface.

now. So you are to be witnesses of the kingdom and its power from here to the very ends of the earth."[107]

John Stott, in his book, *The Spirit, the Church and the World*, ties the Spirit and the kingdom together in a preliminary fashion, but never explores their relationship in depth:

> Two main topics of conversation…were the kingdom of God and the Spirit of God. It seems probable that he also related them to each other, for certainly the prophets had often associated them. Isa. 32:15; 35:6; 43:19; Ezk. 11:19; 36:26-27; 37:11; 39:29; Joel 2:28-29.[108]

Stott adds that obviously the kingdom of God is spiritual, but also "it has radical political and social implications."[109] And, in a brief discussion from Acts 28:31, Stott notes that there may be a difference between the kingdom of God and Jesus Christ (two separate but interrelated parts), but he does not specify what that distinction is. Nor has any other evangelical theologian that I know about.

In Matthew and Mark, Jesus begins his ministry by declaring, "Repent, for the kingdom of God is at hand." Luke's statement doesn't specifically mention the kingdom, but Luke 4:18-19 describes the kingdom with four key concepts: the Spirit, the poor, the oppressed and Jubilee justice. Scattered throughout the gospels are many teachings about the kingdom of God. Then Jesus is crucified and he rises from the dead. The teaching on the kingdom ceases? Not quite! After his resurrection and before his ascension, Jesus continues to teach about the kingdom (Acts 1:3). No wonder his disciples asked him if now was the time for the kingdom to be restored to Israel.

---

[107] Snyder 11.

[108] John Stott, *The Spirit, the Church and the World* (Downers Grove, IL: InterVarsity Press, 1990) 8.

[109] Stott 157.

The kingdom takes center stage in the book of Acts. When Philip preached the gospel in Samaria, this is how it was described in Acts 8:12: "Philip preached the good news of the kingdom of God and the name of Jesus Christ." Then Paul spoke to the Jews in Rome, "testifying to the kingdom of God and trying to convince them about Jesus Christ from the law of Moses and from the prophets" (Acts 28:23). Most Jews rejected this message, so Paul turned to the Gentiles (28:31), "preaching the kingdom of God and teaching about the Lord Jesus Christ."

This is how Paul described the kingdom of God in Romans 14:17:

> The kingdom of God is…justice, shalom and joy in the Holy Spirit. (Noble paraphrase. The NEB translates *dikaiosune* as justice in this passage.)

If you compare the Messianic passages, which are about the kingdom, with Luke 4:18-19, which are about the kingdom, and Romans 14:17, you will find a common emphasis on justice for the poor and oppressed. So I see these passages from Acts on the kingdom and Jesus Christ this way. When the kingdom was being preached, the message highlighted justice. When Jesus Christ was being preached, the message highlighted justification by faith based on the cross and resurrection. So Philip and Paul were preaching a two-pronged gospel: the kingdom and Jesus, justification by faith and justice. Only if we preach and practice this two-pronged gospel do we have comprehensive good news for the poor and oppressed.

The Four-Pronged Gospel Applied

Or maybe we should talk about a four-pronged gospel: the cross, the resurrection, the kingdom of God, and the Holy Spirit. All four are mentioned together in Acts 1:3-5. In Lawndale, Chicago, Wayne Gordon and his colleagues have combined the cross, the resurrection, the Holy Spirit and kingdom justice to transform a poor, urban, ethnic minority community. Listen to Ron Sider's description of this Christian Community Development ministry which combines both quality and quantity; Lawndale was once one of the poorest ghettos in America:

> Over the past twenty years Lawndale Community Church's social ministries have grown into a $10-million-a-year holistic program. They have built or remodeled millions of dollars of low-income housing. The health clinic has twenty-two full-time doctors. The college prep program has assisted and enabled one hundred Lawndale youth to graduate from college. Fifty of them have returned to inner-city Lawndale to offer the same hope to their younger siblings and friends that LCC gave to them. The health clinic is so successful (even though the doctors receive only one-third of a typical doctor's salary) that the infant mortality rate has dropped by 60 percent, making headlines in Chicago newspapers. The federal health officials in the Chicago region came to LCC to ask if they could fund some of LCC's enormously successful programs. Now the federal office requires all its regional staff to read Wayne Gordon's book (*Real Hope in Chicago*).
>
> Why is LCC so successful? There are many reasons: outstanding leadership, good funding, help from the Chicago Bears. According to Wayne Gordon, however, the single most important reason for their success is faith. "None of this would work the way it does," Wayne says, "apart from the vibrant faith in Christ that motivates all our staff and the active relational evangelism that has led hundreds and hundreds of Lawndale residents to personal faith and transformed lives."[110]

I am afraid that the majority of America's 60,000,000 evangelicals are too busy chasing the American dream to be actively

---

[110] Ronald J. Sider, *Just Generosity: A New Vision for Overcoming Poverty in America*, 2nd Ed. (Grand Rapids, MI: Baker Books, 2007) 279-280.

concerned about our poor urban ghettos. But I would hazard a guess that 6,000,000 of them are ready and willing to be involved. All they need is someone to show them the way. I would like to issue a clarion call based on Luke 4:18-19 to these 6,000,000 to help us incarnate the kingdom of God among the millions of poor in America. In the epilogue to this book, Dr. John Perkins will share about new ways that the Perkins Foundation is seeking to connect the resources of the Church to communities of need; if you are one of the 6,000,000 evangelicals ready to respond, listen carefully to his vision to see what your role might be.

The four-pronged gospel has been taken to Fond-des-Blancs, Haiti, by Jean and Joy Thomas. In the late 1970s, Jean had a four-year internship with John Perkins in Jackson, Mississippi. The three "R's" of Christian Community Development – relocation, reconciliation and redistribution – became part of the marrow of his bones. Voice of Calvary Fellowship sent Jean and Joy back to Haiti as their missionaries around 1980. After 20 years of CCD ministry in Haiti, Jean and Joy wrote a book, describing what God had done in Fond-des-Blancs, entitled *At Home with the Poor.*[111]

A few years ago, a hurricane hit one city in Haiti, and the resulting flood wiped out major sections. I was in Seattle at the time. The *Seattle Times* devoted one page, three articles, to a description of Haiti. I don't think there was a single positive word in the three articles. They were an endless litany of complex, interrelated, unsolvable problems. Terribly bad news. But Jean and Joy and their Haitian colleagues have tackled most of those "unsolvable" problems and made good progress toward solving many of them. So this is a remarkable story of what can happen if the cross, the resurrection, the Spirit and kingdom justice are combined and implemented by wise, loving leaders. I visited Haiti about 10 years ago; these are my reflections:

---

[111] Jean Thomas, *At Home with the Poor* (Newberg, OR: Barclay Press, 2003).

Lowell Noble

After visiting Fond-des-Blancs, Haiti, in March of 1998, a time of drought, I am reminded of two Scriptural images:

The people who sat in darkness have seen a great light.

They drank the water of life freely.

Fond-des-Blancs, a rural, isolated, mountainous region in southern Haiti, is an area of severe poverty and illiteracy. Before Jean and Joy arrived in the early 1980s, the people did not have access to clean water. I recall with joy a simple sight – a four-pronged spigot out of which flows a generous supply of clean water. Pure enough for me, an outsider, to drink.

From early morning to late evening, a steady stream of people from up to five miles around come to get cups or gallons of precious, clean water. Small children carry a plastic gallon of water; women carry a five-gallon pail on their heads; donkeys carry saddlebags full of water. Occasionally a truck will stop and fill up many barrels of water. Women wash clothes nearby. Even after three years of partial drought, the capped spring is still flowing, providing a plentiful, though diminished, supply of water.

When Jean (Haitian) and Joy (American) Thomas arrived in Fond-des-Blancs, they asked the people what their number one priority was; the people replied, "an accessible supply of clean water." They found a nearby spring. The Thomases told the people that they would supply the cement to cap the spring and the pipe to bring the water one-half mile downstream, if the people would supply the labor. Sometimes digging through solid rock with hand tools, the people worked hard to bring the water down to a nearby road. This cooperative effort built a strong sense of **community** and a belief that they could tackle any project and succeed. The water project also illustrates this kingdom principle: As God sends the rain on the just and the unjust, so this clean water project was for Christians and non-Christians alike. It was a way for God's people to demonstrate God's concern for all who are in need.

The spiritual water of life is also flowing freely. A vigorous mother church of 250 members has spawned twelve satellite churches, all staffed by Haitian pastors. Each of these remote churches also has a small school.

Over the years, under Jean's guidance, indigenous leaders have carried out a number of projects: millions of trees planted on denuded, eroded hills and mountains; a new breed of pigs to replace disease-ridden old pigs; a quality primary school serving 300 students; a road-building project of around 100 miles using indigenous hand labor; and a thriving credit union as an alternative to loan sharks. All of these projects were built around a strong sense of community nurtured by intentional cooperative efforts.

To learn more about this remarkable story of kingdom building in a dirt-poor, rural community, call 601-354-1563 for a copy of *At Home with the Poor* or visit www.hcdf.org.

We began this book by referring to the current ethical dilemma facing our country – the 10-1 wealth gap. This is grossly unfair – a justice issue that the church is not addressing on a large scale. This is more than a political issue to be debated on a partisan basis. This is a **Biblical justice issue.** So my following suggestions are not made on a partisan political basis, though I know that many of my readers may be tempted to see them as such. Try your best to see them through a Biblical lens.

1. In 2010, the massive Bush tax cuts for the rich will expire, unless renewed by a vote of Congress. These tax cuts widened the wealth gap between the rich and the poor. The evangelical church should mount a large lobbying effort to make sure that these tax cuts are not renewed.

2. In terms of health care, there are 47,000,000 uninsured persons in our country. As a justice issue, we need universal health care. A recent *U.S. News and World Report*

article[112] stated that Britain delivers universal health care to all of its citizens at half the cost per person when compared to the U.S. Not only do the poor have access to health care, but the British infant mortality rate is lower than ours, and their life expectancy is higher than ours. The British approach would be more just than our health care system is. Many people think that a universal health care system would be prohibitively expensive. It need not be if we follow the British model. Per capita health care costs in Britain are $2,546 whereas in the U.S., per capita costs are $6,102. Our present model for health care is the one that is prohibitively expensive. Would this motto sell universal health care? "Reduce costs by one-half; go universal." And be more just. Sounds like a bargain to me.

3. According to another article[113] in the same issue of *U.S. News*, Finland has a better educational system than does the U.S. One reason: all teachers are required to have a masters degree. And Finland makes a big investment in teacher education as well as programs that support children and families at an early age. Quality education for all children is a justice issue; the church should vigorously support such efforts.

4. This will be the most controversial suggestion, but I believe that it is a justice issue. Cut military spending by one-half. Our present budget is around $300 billion. One hundred fifty billion dollars would be plenty of money for a defensive army, but not enough to engage in unwise wars such as Vietnam and Iraq. Fifty billion dollars

---

[112] Thomas Grose, "Free Health Care For All," *U.S. News and World Report* 16 Mar./2 Apr. 2007: 66.
[113] Lisa Moore, "The Secret to Smarter Schools," *U.S. News and World Report* 16 Mar./2 Apr. 2007: 54.

of the savings should be spent on fighting the war on terror by doing good around the world. You do not win the hearts and minds of a people through the barrel of a gun. Another $50 billion should be spent on restitution to Native Americans and Afro Americans, providing things such as college scholarships and down payment assistance on homes. The other $50 billion, you decide.

Conclusion: We can have a more just society, reduce the wealth gap, by our churches getting heavily involved in rebuilding poor communities. We can have a more just society by changing some of our national priorities; some of these changes will save money, some will cost more money, but all of them could be done without breaking the bank. I'm sure that you can come up with other ideas. God is concerned about the poor and oppressed, and we should be deeply concerned as well.

I urge you, as you are coming to the end of this book, to move beyond simply reading about these issues. There are many things you can do to work for justice in our society. You can choose one of the four issues I just mentioned, and invite others to join you in advocacy efforts toward just laws. You can visit our online forum (http://www.urban-verses.com/O2JJ/), dialog with others who are concerned about the poor and oppressed, and help build a network of Kingdom builders. While you're online, you can look into various internship opportunities for hands-on experience. Or, you can add to the conversation by writing one of these books, which I believe the American Church needs desperately:

1. A Biblical, historical and sociological examination of ethnocentrism/oppression.
2. A theology built around the Spirit, the poor, the oppressed and Jubilee justice tied to the four-pronged gospel of the cross, the resurrection, the Holy Spirit and the kingdom of God as justice.

Whatever you do, do it prayerfully, after searching the Scriptures, in the power and under the guidance of the Holy Spirit. Let us do justice, that we might see God's Kingdom come, on earth as it is in Heaven, and experience His Shalom in our communities!

Approach of the King

One would think
When the King drew near
That His subjects would fall silent
Bow down
Then humbly inquire,
"Who, Lord, are we to be?"
"What, Lord, are we to do?"
"How, Lord, are we to live?"

Instead, we quarrel and fight
Raising our voices
In an ever-escalating contest
To see who can proclaim the loudest,
"This is the way –
The King will bless it by and by –
So come, follow me."

Epilogue

by John Perkins

Luke 4:18-19 and the Mississippi Delta: The Jubilee Justice Decade

The Story of Ruth

Ruth is a part of the folklore of the John Perkins Foundation. As a student at Seattle Pacific University (SPU), Ruth came to Jackson, Mississippi, on a mission team. She was profoundly moved by what she saw, experienced and was taught here.

Ruth went back to SPU and convinced the University's President, Philip Eaton, to come down with the next SPU mission team. President Eaton was also profoundly moved by his experience in Jackson; he then initiated the Perkins Center for Reconciliation and Community Development at SPU.

After Ruth graduated from SPU, she returned to Mississippi. She is now teaching math to 8th graders in Clarksdale. One of the best and brightest is serving among the poorest of the poor in the Delta.

Ruth, I applaud your dedication and commitment. You have responded to the leading of the Holy Spirit. This is very good, but there is still something missing. The mission that you are on needs a team, a church, behind you, supporting you. How about a small house church made up of other SPU students/graduates under the guidance of a SPU professor? This team, working with local indigenous leadership, could dedicate themselves to long-term spiritual and social change in the Delta.

The Delta:
The Pre-Civil Rights Period

The land was rich. The oppression was dehumanizing. The poverty was severe. The white evangelical church was missing in action.

On a 1000-acre plantation, an owner needed around 200 hands to plant, chop and pick cotton. The wealth of Mississippi was in the Delta. Political power, the control of the state legislature, flowed out of the Delta. The U.S. Senators from Mississippi saw to it that federal agricultural subsidies flowed into the Delta. Oppression ran deep and was highly organized.

What about the black church? Was it a force for justice? Jackson-area preachers would truck workers from the capital to the plantations to work. In the Delta, the black church was often located on the plantation. The white plantation owner would give the black preacher $5.00 for preaching. The owner controlled, to some degree, the black church. No call to stop oppression would come from the black pulpit while the white plantation owner was in charge.

Black public school teachers were also highly controlled. A prospective teacher who wanted a job had to go through the white county supervisor and the white superintendent to be hired. The teachers dared not challenge the system in any way, or they would lose their jobs.

The white church taught that Blacks were inferior, cursed by God, descendants of Ham, destined to be hewers of wood and drawers of water. So the white church endorsed, supported the system of oppression; they gave it religious sanction.

And there was no justice for Blacks in the criminal justice system. That system was part of the system of oppression.

Overall, both the black and white churches were more a part of the problem than a part of the solution. Lee Harper, an Afro-American woman born and raised in the Delta, asserts:

Injustice ran deep and cloaked itself well among those things that appeared just.

Religion gave cover for oppression.

The Delta in 1989

In 1989, a federal government commission reported that the lower Mississippi Delta, including parts of Mississippi, Louisiana, Arkansas, Missouri, Tennessee, Kentucky and Illinois, was the poorest region in the U.S. The *Wall Street Journal* sent a staff reporter, Dennis Farney, down to do a story on this poverty-stricken region. The front-page headlines blared:

River of Despair
Along the Rich Banks
of the Mississippi Live
Poorest of U.S. Poor

They Endure a Lack of Jobs
and a Plantation Mentality,
While Landowners Thrive

Where Dreams of Blacks Die

Farney reported:

For here is a region that epitomizes the extremes of American wealth and poverty. It is almost unbelievably fertile, with topsoil 25 feet thick or more. It has mansions and big cars and a wealthy gentry that for decades has gathered round the fountain in the ornate lobby of Memphis's grand old Peabody Hotel... But, especially along

the Mississippi, it has county rates of poverty that range
from 20% to 50% plus... What the Delta doesn't have is a
stabilizing middle class.[114]

A medical doctor, Dr. Lamm, shares with Farney about the
types of diseases she sees: "These are the kinds of things you
see in Haiti or Mexico, not in the United States."

From this article, it is clear that widespread poverty persists
in the Delta. At the same time, it is important to note that some
significant changes *have* occurred. The Klan is no longer terror-
izing the population. The right to vote exists. Primary education
is available on a broader basis. There has been some improve-
ment in health care. But even with this progress, the situation is
still pitiful for poor Blacks.

Most public schools are still highly segregated. With a few
exceptions, the majority are 99% segregated. In the late 1960s,
the federal government ordered all public schools in Mississippi
to be desegregated. To avoid integration, Whites set up private
schools – academies. Even in the capital city of Jackson, most
public school are 95% segregated today.

When the IRS discovered that the reason these private
schools were set up was to avoid integration, it revoked their
tax-exempt status. So Whites then turned the private academies
over to the church; the federal government could not touch the
church. The Baptist church became the guardian of segregation
in Mississippi and the Delta.

The private academies were adequately funded by Whites,
but the black public schools were underfunded. Separate and
unequal education reigns in the Delta today.

Conclusion: The schools are segregated. The church is segregated. The church is not releasing the Delta poor from
oppression. The church is not incarnating Jubilee justice in poor
communities in the Delta.

---

[114] Dennis Farney, "River of Despair," *The Wall Street Journal*
(Vol. LXX, No. 254) 19 Oct. 1989.

From Katrina to the Delta

The church's response to Hurricane Katrina has been magnificent – the church's finest hour. Thousands of volunteers and millions of dollars have poured into the Mississippi Gulf Coast. There are hundreds of heart-warming stories to be told. The church responded beautifully to a **natural catastrophe**.

But, by comparison, the church's response to the ongoing, generational, **social catastrophe** in the Delta has been pitifully inadequate.

We now know, based on the response to Katrina, that the American church has the capacity to respond to the Delta social catastrophe. So here is our challenge, our strategy for that response. We invite you to join with us.

The Jubilee Justice Decade: A Dream for the Delta

In 1964, Afro-American leaders in Mississippi initiated a bold strategy to break the back of legal segregation in the state. This strategy was dubbed Freedom Summer. These leaders recruited 1,000 northern volunteers to join them in the battle for freedom. The strategy was successful, but sadly it was implemented without the participation of a significant number of evangelicals.

Guess who did respond? Over 600 Jews, mostly "secular Jews" – that is, Jews who were agnostic or atheistic, but who had a passion for justice.

This time we want to issue a call for evangelicals to participate in a 10-year Jubilee Justice program. We propose to identify 10 Delta communities where there is some indigenous leadership that would welcome a partnership with 10 concerned evangelicals who would relocate to assist with the rebuilding of their communities.

Each community would be paired with a seminary or a Christian liberal arts college or university. Participating schools would recruit the 10 interns from among their students, graduates or retired alumni. Each year, a faculty member would be assigned to the chosen community. Over a period of 10 years, 10 different faculty members would serve.

For example, Ruth and SPU would choose a Delta community. Together they would develop a house church or join a progressive church in the community. Working with the indigenous leadership, they would develop a long-term strategy to improve the community.

The John Perkins Foundation will undergird this program with teaching, networking and resources; we will also work to bring in the support and expertise of other organizations, such as Habitat for Humanity; World Vision, U.S.A.; and Kids Across America.

We would look to the Holy Spirit and seek his anointing to preach good news to the Delta poor. We seek the anointing of the Holy Spirit to release the Delta oppressed. We seek the power and wisdom of the Holy Spirit to incarnate Jubilee Justice in Delta communities.

Jesus told his followers to pray that God's Kingdom would come on earth as it is in Heaven. Will you help us in our efforts to build the Kingdom in Mississippi?

Jubilee

When the trumpet sounds
Its melody of justice
Its harmony of grace
Its refrain of hope
Its song of shalom

Forty-nine long years
Of trial and hardship
Poverty and loss
Become but momentary afflictions
Counting as nothing
Compared to the joy
Set before
And now come upon
The people of God

For more information about the Jubilee Justice Decade
contact the John Perkins Foundation at
601-354-1563 (phone)
601-352-6882 (fax)
jmpfoffice@jam.rr.com
1831 Robinson Street
Jackson MS 39209
www.jmpf.org

To order additional copies of this book, and/or to participate
in the Oppression to Jubilee Justice online forum, visit
www.urban-verses.com/O2JJ/
or call 601-209-2211

To learn more about the Haiti Christian Development Fund,
go to www.hcdf.org